UNDERSTANDING ASSISTANCE DOGS

UNDERSTANDING ASSISTANCE DOGS

IS AN ASSISTANCE DOG THE RIGHT TOOL FOR YOU?

JENNIFER GRAVROK, PHD

For more information, email understandingassistancedogs@gmail.com

ISBN: 979-8-89109-185-6 - paperback
ISBN: 979-8-89109-272-3 - hardcover
ISBN: 979-8-89109-186-3 - ebook

CONTENTS

PART 3: SO, YOU BELIEVE AN ASSISTANCE DOG IS THE RIGHT TOOL FOR YOU. NOW WHAT?

PREFACE

Social media portrays the benefits of an assistance dog rampantly. It is also commonly portrayed that having an assistance dog will make everything better. As much as I wish this were the case, it is not. I completed my PhD in 2019, having studied the benefits and challenges that first-time assistance dog handlers experience when working with their assistance dog. My research and subsequent years in the industry have shown me that handlers who are prepared for the journey, with realistic expectations, will experience fewer challenges initially and reap more long-term success as a handler/assistance dog team than those who don't have these understandings.

Success is possible. You want to be *successful* with an assistance dog, right? To experience long-term success, it is important, I truly believe, that you fully understand what the journey involves. Just like in any journey, there will be highs and lows, bumps that cause you to stumble and backtrack or launch you forward. All of which should be expected throughout this journey.

It will take a lot of work to be successful with an assistance dog, but the benefits can be life changing. With success, you can manage your disability easier, be more independent, and feel safe and secure in public or your own home again. Success also brings feelings of unconditional love and support from your dog. For many people, an assistance dog can change their lives in incredible ways.

Unsuccessful teams, in contrast, will experience more difficult challenges that can extend for the next ten or more years. Although their dog may provide benefits, handlers may wind up dedicating too much energy and effort to them. Or the dog may require too many "spoons" (activities, interactions, or other energy-depleting situations) each day. Consequently, the handlers may accomplish less daily or perhaps need extra assistance with their dog and therefore are more dependent than without a dog.

I urge you not to rush into this decision but to take it seriously, as it is not just about you and your success, but also about the life of another living being. Therefore, it is important that you are completely honest with yourself when asking, "Is the journey to working with an assistance dog the right choice for me currently?"

Irrespective of your (current) response, I commend you for starting your learning process now, because even if right now is not the right time for you to start working with an assistance dog, you are preparing yourself to potentially take that step in the future. However, if you aren't truthful with yourself about your abilities and expected challenges and start this journey without fully learning and understanding if it is right for you, then sooner or later, often too late, you will realize your mistake. Too often this occurs after you've invested your heart, time, and money into this journey only to determine that it wasn't an appropriate time to start or the appropriate choice.

I have worked with many of these assistance dog handlers who didn't make the right choice, and they all have one thing in common: a lack of initial understanding of what it will *really* take to successfully work with an assistance dog. To prevent this from happening to you, my goal is to use my years of research and work in this field to help you understand as much as possible about this journey upfront. I aim to help you understand if an assistance dog is the right tool for you.

This book is divided into three main sections. Part 1 focuses on whether an assistance dog will be able to assist with your disability. Part 2 will help you determine if your lifestyle will enable you to form a mutually beneficial relationship with an assistance dog. Part 3 focuses on the various considerations for how to acquire an assistance dog.

Because an assistance dog is not the right tool for everyone, Parts One and Two provide incredibly important information in making that determination. An assistance dog needs both a job to do (Part 1) and a mutually beneficial partnership (Part 2). Moving on to Part 3, if you have determined that an assistance dog *is* the right tool for you, here I help you think through which method of acquiring an assistance dog will lead to the highest chance of success. As you read, I will lead you through the process of examining whether you can realistically and successfully incorporate an assistance dog into your life to receive the benefits you need, in a way that enables the assistance dog to live a happy life.

To further assist you, I illustrate with examples (that may or may not be relevant to your situation). Since each handler is unique and each dog is unique, take time to view the examples through your own lens. You know your situation and the impacts of your disability on living the life you want to. It is impossible to cover every situation that could occur for each type of assistance dog, but more of it will be relevant to you than you might initially think. Additionally, it can take some soul-searching and honest conversations with people in your support network, but I truly believe that if you *honestly* work through this book, you will be able to answer the question as to whether working with an assistance dog is right for you.

Throughout, I provide important discussion questions (involving your supporters), thought prompts (things for you to respond to), and places to make action plans (start the work now). Utilize these! As you read, take notes in the margins, use a highlighter, break the binding (I encourage you to!), and use this book in any way whatsoever that works for you. Make yourself at home in the book. Share the information with the supporters in your life. You are on the path to success.

🐾 Right now, write out a list of pros and cons of working with an assistance dog and continue to refine it as you read. The next page is intentionally blank so you can use this space for that purpose. I encourage you to rip out the page and use it as your bookmark as you read so it's easily accessible to add to your list.

PROS	CONS

PROS	CONS

Part 1

Can an assistance dog assist with your disability?

Incorporating an assistance dog into your life is a big decision, one that Jane did not take lightly, and neither should you. Jane, a young adult, commonly experiences "bad days" where pain, stiffness, or soreness greatly limit or prevent her from doing basic activities of daily living like bending to pick things up, putting on shoes and socks, or doing the laundry. On these days she needs the support of a cane to get around safely. On other days, Jane has less pain, stiffness, or soreness and seems more "normal."

When Jane came to me, she questioned whether she was "disabled enough" to need an assistance dog. She had heard all the wonderful stories about how assistance dogs can help people with disabilities, but the anecdotes focused on people who appeared more disabled than she was. Discouraged, she believed that for her to work with an assistance dog, every day had to be a "bad day." After discussing her disability, lifestyle, and other key factors with her, it became apparent to me that she had enough bad-pain days that the dog would have a sufficient amount of work to do in helping to mitigate her pain.

However, once working with her assistance dog, Jane realized how much she also needed a dog on the days she was mostly "normal"—for instance, having Rex pick up dropped things even on these days meant that she had enough energy left over to be able to cook dinner independently. This, she hadn't been able to do for years, even on her best days, as by the end of the day, she was exhausted, hoping she hadn't overdone it, making tomorrow a bad-pain day. With the help of her assistance dog Rex, Jane now lives a much more fulfilling life.

Just like Jane did, the very first step in your assistance dog journey, as with any venture, is deciding whether you want to begin. As this particular journey is life changing and—not to forget—involves another living being, you must take both of you into account to ensure it will be mutually beneficial.

Assistance dogs rely on a mutually beneficial partnership to be successful in their role. Determining if you can realistically form a mutually beneficial partnership with an assistance dog is difficult in the abstract, especially if you have never lived or worked with one before. Throughout the book, I will describe the qualities necessary for creating this relationship. To determine if you will be able to provide this, you also need clear information regarding the journey and your responsibilities. My goal is to support your efforts in making an informed decision.

Do you know the terminology associated with assistance animals? We will unwrap that in Chapter 1. The assistance dog industry is full of words that are similar yet distinct. Making it even more complicated, frequently the general public and the media use this vocabulary incorrectly. You will learn about commonly mistaken terminology, different categories of assistance dogs, and how to identify what disabilities or conditions each dog assists with.

Then, in Chapter 2 we will move to a discussion of what skills assistance dogs can be trained to provide. You are most likely exploring the option of working with one because of the benefits medical professionals have told you about or stories you heard in the media. Trained benefits are incredibly important, as through them an assistance dog mitigates the effects of the handler's disability.

Finally, the third chapter will cover the *untrained* benefits assistance dogs can provide—typically categorized as physical, psychological, and social benefits.

Part 1 Learning Objectives

By the end of reading Part 1, you will be able to…

- differentiate between commonly used terminology.
- identify the eight types of assistance dogs based on the common disabilities they assist with.
- describe why an assistance dog is, in this framework, a piece of medical equipment.
- list common physical skills that each type of assistance dog can perform.
- recognize realistic and unrealistic expectations regarding physical skills for an assistance dog.
- describe the psychological and social benefits and how they arise.

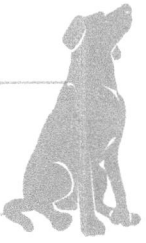

CHAPTER 1

What is an assistance dog?

Assistance dogs, also known as service dogs in the United States, are dogs who are trained to perform specific work or trained tasks to mitigate their handler's disability. As they are trained to high behavior standards, they are allowed access to public spaces with their handler.

Important terminology

The terms "assistance dog" and "service dog" are interchangeable in the United States. Internationally, however, "service dog" commonly describes a dog that provides a service or work but not necessarily for someone with a disability. For example, a dog who works in the military, with police, or does detection work is commonly considered a service dog.

Internationally speaking, "assistance dog" is the preferred term. Additionally, the international accrediting association for high-quality assistance dog organizations, Assistance Dogs International, uses the term "assistance dog." For consistency, this book will speak in terms of "assistance dog" throughout.

If you are used to the term "service dog" in reference to dogs who assist people with disabilities, substitute it in your mind interchangeably with assistance dog.

The person in control, overseeing the work of the assistance dog, is "the handler." In most cases, the handler is also the person who receives the trained benefits from the assistance dog to mitigate their disability. One exception is where the person the dog is directly assisting in mitigating their disability is too young or not cognitively capable of managing the dog on their own. This often occurs with young children with autism or diabetes, where a parent or primary carer is the handler.

An assistance dog working in conjunction with the handler is considered a team. An assistance dog working with a handler but providing benefits to a different person with disabilities (who is young or not cognitively capable) is considered a triad team because three individuals are involved. Throughout this book, unless otherwise specified, we will assume the handler is the person with a disability receiving benefits from the assistance dog.

There are two common terms that assistance dogs, or service dogs, commonly get confused with: "emotional support animals" (ESAs) and "therapy dogs." This confusion arises because each of these types of dogs falls within the overarching "assistance animal" category. ESAs and therapy dogs, however, are distinct in their training, in whom they provide benefits to and where they are legally allowed to accompany a person.

An emotional support animal provides benefits to people with a mental health diagnosis from a licensed mental health professional. These animals (not necessarily dogs) require no formal training. Therefore, they do not perform a specific *trained* task. The benefits arise solely from the companionship and comfort they offer. Due to the lack of required training, emotional support animals are not allowed in public except in dog-friendly locations. Within the United States under the Fair Housing Act, they are required to be allowed in their companion's housing accommodations, as are assistance dogs even if they lie outside of the pet policy rules in relation to species, size, or breed.

Although emotional support animals don't provide trained skills for their handler, they do provide benefits. Commonly, people who realize that an assistance dog is *not* the right tool for them may instead realize that, with a much lower barrier to entry, an emotional support animal can provide the benefits they seek. Keep this in mind if you realize in reading this book that an assistance dog is not the right tool for you.

Therapy dogs, in contrast, have been trained to perform skills that can assist many people, including those with a disability. Their skills can be similar to assistance dog skills. However, they are also trained to interact with many people. This is not the case for assistance dogs, who are trained to assist only one person for their specific needs.

In the case of the therapy dog, the handler, rather than receiving benefits, is providing the dog as a service to others. These handlers and dogs often need to attend classes and be tested and verified before working with their target population.

Therapy dogs are also different from assistance dogs in that they perform their specifically trained skills in designated settings—places like hospitals, nursing homes, clinics, schools, etc. At these locations, the therapy dog handler and the business have an agreement for the dog to provide the service. Therefore, therapy dogs are not allowed, without permission, in the general public.

Although assistance dogs could technically also be therapy dogs, as they have trained skills they could provide anyone, not just their specific handler, this is *not* recommended. Primarily because an assistance dog should work *for one person only*. By working as a therapy dog, they tend to be very solicitous, eager to help everyone. This inclination can cause conflict in the dog, creating challenges for the handler when the dog is in the assistance dog role.

Do not get an assistance dog and expect them also to do therapy dog work. This is not fair, as it can send the dog mixed messages. It also adds more work for the dog. Therefore, it is strongly recommended to allow assistance dogs to do their one job as assistance dogs and do it well, rather than do poorly at two jobs.

This book will not discuss emotional support animals or therapy dogs further.

🐾 What is the difference in training between an assistance dog, emotional support animal, and therapy dog?

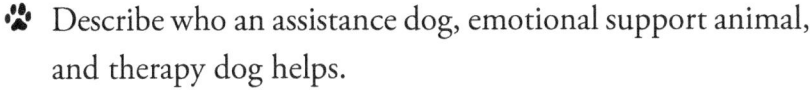

Describe who an assistance dog, emotional support animal, and therapy dog helps.

Where in public can an assistance dog, emotional support animal, and therapy dog go?

Types of assistance dogs

There are eight primary types of assistance dogs. These currently include, in no particular order, guide dogs, mobility assistance dogs, diabetic alert dogs, seizure response/alert dogs, hearing alert dogs, autism assistance dogs, psychiatric assistance dogs, and medical alert dogs. I use the word "currently" because as we better understand all the ways dogs can be trained to help people and assist with various disabilities, I believe that the types of assistance dogs will grow to meet the needs of an expanded set of disabilities.

Next, I will describe whom each type of assistance dog can assist, offering general information about each job. The specific skills they perform will be discussed later.

Guide Dogs (aka, seeing eye dogs or leader dogs) assist people with vision impairment or who are blind. They guide their handler through busy locations and around obstacles that they could otherwise trip over or run into. They also lead them to practiced locations, such as bus stops or coffee shops. However, the handler doesn't follow the dog thoughtlessly; handlers must know where they are in space and have accurate orientation and mobility skills to work with a guide dog. This typically involves a requirement to be proficient in using a white cane.

Part of the guide dog's job is to assist the handler in safely crossing the street from corner to corner, preventing the handler from accidentally veering into the road or traffic. Contrary to popular belief, guide dogs don't tell their handler when it is safe to cross the road. Rather, it is up to the handler to determine that by listening to the traffic. If the dog disagrees with this decision—for instance, seeing a car approaching—then they can perform intelligent disobedience, refusing to guide.

Mobility Assistance Dogs help with mobility challenges. These dogs assist the widest variety of disabilities—anything involving limitations in moving, bending, grasping, walking, range of motion, etc. Common disability diagnosis includes cerebral palsy, muscular dystrophy, multiple sclerosis, Parkinson's, amputees, postural orthostatic tachycardia syndrome (POTS),

Ehlers-Danlos syndrome, complex regional pain syndrome, etc.; it also includes paraplegics, quadriplegics, and more.

Mobility assistance dogs also typically have the widest variety of physical tasks that they can provide their handler. These skills primarily revolve around assisting with activities of daily living like opening/closing doors, helping with the laundry or with getting undressed. Although mobility assistance dogs have the capacity to perform the widest variety of skills, they only perform the ones necessary to their handler. This means that even though a mobility dog can be trained to perform a particular skill, it doesn't mean a particular mobility dog is trained to do so. For example, a person who doesn't need help with laundry doesn't need a dog trained to assist with laundry.

Diabetic Alert Dogs assist people with diabetes who experience rapid and unsafe changes in blood glucose levels or hypo/hyperglycemic unawareness. As hypoglycemia is typically more dangerous than hyperglycemia, sometimes the dogs are only trained to alert to their handler's low blood sugar.

Sensitive to the change in scent the handler produces, diabetic alert dogs alert their handler to dangerous or rapid changes in blood glucose levels or when their blood sugar is out of range. When the dogs notice this scent change, they are trained to give an alert in a specific way—often accomplished through a nose nudge or paw touch to the handler's body. A handler who receives this alert then has the job of checking their blood sugar level to determine if their dog is right and what to do to correct the blood sugar level.

After alerting, the assistance dog can also provide response skills, such as retrieving their handler's testing kit or retrieving juice or glucose tabs to assist in the process of bringing their handler's blood sugar back to normal range; the dog can also be trained to get help for their handler, which I will discuss later.

Seizure Response Dogs, or Seizure Alert Dogs (also known as seizure assist dogs) assist people who have various seizure disorders. As the research is still evolving, it is not conclusively understood how dogs can alert before a seizure occurs, or what cues or biological markers they are picking up on. Therefore, seizure alert dogs are very difficult to train, so they are commonly initially placed as seizure response dogs.

Seizure response dogs are trained to *respond* to a seizure by providing benefits to their handler during or after a seizure, *not before*. This can include going to get help within the home or pressing an emergency button. They can also provide tactile stimulation such as licking, nudging, or providing deep pressure therapy, which may lessen the duration of the seizure by interrupting it. Additionally, after the seizure the dog can help their handler reorient to the environment more quickly.

A seizure response dog can sometimes become a seizure alert dog. This change may occur if the trained seizure response dog begins to show signs that they know a seizure is about to happen. These signs are often called *pre-alert behaviors* and can include normal stress behaviors or staring at the handler. The behaviors they display indicating they believe a seizure is about to occur, when identified, can then be fostered through new and continued training to possibly develop into an alert.

Not all seizure response dogs will have the awareness of or desire to alert.

Currently, it's impossible to know whether a seizure response dog will pick up on a specific person's seizure activity, or if the dog will have the desire to alert to seizures before they occur, so alert work is often not guaranteed.

Hearing Alert Dogs assist people who are Deaf or hard of hearing. They alert their handler to specific sounds in the environment so they can respond to them or keep themselves safe. Similar to diabetic alert dogs, these dogs are trained to get their handler's attention in specific ways when they hear a sound they are trained to respond to. For example, they might alert their handler to the fire alarm, doorbell, timers/alarms, or other particular sounds such as their baby crying.

For handlers who wear hearing aids or cochlear implants, alerts are especially important when their hearing-assist technology is not in use. This could be for reasons such as showering, or sleeping, for stimulation reasons, or ear health requirements, when batteries are dead, etc., as in these situations the handler is receiving much less auditory information.

Autism Assistance Dogs assist people on the autism spectrum. Though adults can also utilize autism assistance dogs, most are trained to assist children with an autism spectrum diagnosis. As many of these teams involve a child receiving benefit from the assistance dog, often a parent or other adult carer needs to act as the handler and primarily, or in conjunction with the child, controls the dog. As mentioned, these situations create triad teams.

Autism assistance dogs are frequently trained to interrupt self-stimming (unwanted or potentially harmful repetitive) behaviors such as hand flapping or nail biting, or to provide deep-pressure therapy. Especially important for children, autism assistance dogs can help keep a child safe in public by preventing them from eloping or providing a grounding presence. In triad teams, the handler can also, in various situations, use the dog to redirect a child, thus potentially preventing undesirable behavior. For example, a meltdown at the checkout line; to prevent this, the handler can redirect the child's energy or emotion onto the dog instead of the situation the child finds overwhelming.

Psychiatric Assistance Dogs (sometimes known as PTSD dogs) assist people who have various psychiatric disorders, most commonly post-traumatic stress disorder (PTSD). This is currently the fastest growing type of assistance dog, as it is becoming more recognized and understood what an assistance dog can do to assist people with psychiatric disorders. Commonly misconceived, these dogs are provided *not* only to veterans. They assist civilians as well.

The psychological benefits these dogs are commonly trained to provide for their handler could be skills like turning on lights, watching their back, interrupting repetitive behaviors, identifying and interrupting signs of anxiety, and more. In general, their ability to provide great psychological benefits and feelings of safety are touted as most important to the psychiatric assistance dog handler.

Medical Alert Dog is both an umbrella term and a new category of assistance dog. Diabetes alert dogs and seizure alert dogs fall within the medical alert dog category. However, there are reports of assistance dogs alerting to medical conditions besides seizures and diabetes. This has primarily included (so far) alerting to changes in heart rate, blood pressure, or the presence of a life-threatening allergen. Such dogs have generally been considered medical alert dogs.

The types of assistance dogs will continue to grow in the future as we learn more about how trained dogs can assist people with various disabilities. The examples in this book will not be biased toward one type of assistance dog over another. Many examples will not specifically reference a type of assistance dog, as the experience or principle will be similar irrespective of the assistance dog's skills or the person's disability.

🐾 What type of assistance dog would you benefit from the most?

🐾 Are there other types of assistance dogs that would benefit you? If so, what are they?

Medical equipment

As demonstrated, assistance dogs assist with MANY medical conditions through trained abilities to mitigate the effects of the handler's disability or medical condition. Assistance dogs are, therefore, considered a piece of medical equipment. They are a *tool* to assist with a medical condition or disability.

Traditional assistive devices have one function. A wheelchair assists with movement around a space. A glucose monitor monitors glucose levels. Hearing aids or cochlear implants pick up sounds in the environment. These pieces of medical equipment are great aids to the people who need them; however, they are limited in their functions and are typically specific to a single diagnosis or similar diagnoses.

Compared to most medical equipment, assistance dogs can have a much broader range of functions and disabilities they assist with. For example, an assistance dog can provide both diabetic alerts and mobility assistance or hearing alert and psychiatric assistance, etc. An assistance dog's versatility is incredibly beneficial as a piece of medical equipment and sets them apart from more standard forms of equipment.

Assistance dogs do not, however, *replace* your need for currently prescribed forms of medical equipment. A hearing alert dog does not replace your cochlear implant or hearing aid. A diabetic alert dog will not replace a person with diabetes' need for a CGM. An assistance dog will support and should be used in conjunction with your primary devices or equipment that you are already using, not replace them. A mobility dog should not replace a cane, walker, or other pieces of medical equipment. Commonly, people believe that if they put a harness on their dog, they can rely on the dog for stability rather than a cane or walker. This is not true. An assistance dog should not be utilized like a cane. Placing constant downward pressure on a dog is not good for their physical body or health and, for the wellbeing of the dog, should not be done. Do not expect a dog to take over these functions; rather, use an assistance dog in conjunction with the equipment that has been prescribed.

The only exception to this is for vision impairment. While a blind or impaired-vision handler is using the guide dog, there is no need for a white cane. But guide dog handlers should still be proficient in using the white cane and have strong orientation and mobility skills for times when they are not using the dog.

Assistance dogs can also provide benefits where no comparable device exists. This is true for psychiatric assistance dogs and seizure alert or response dogs, where often there is no other tool available. Therefore, some assistance dogs can provide incredible benefits to their handler that cannot be replicated elsewhere.

An assistance dog is one tool that could *possibly* help mitigate your disability. There may be others out there as well. It is your responsibility to determine if an assistance dog is the right tool for you. Compared to other tools, assistance dogs come with higher stakes because they are living beings that require a lot of care. Compared to other forms of adaptive equipment, they also require a lot of dedicated time, effort, and maintenance to work properly.

🐾 Will an assistance dog replace any of your current medical equipment? Why or why not?

🐾 What benefits and challenges can you add to your list?

CHAPTER 2

Trained benefits

This chapter will walk you through the benefits assistance dogs commonly provide and could *possibly* provide you. Since each assistance dog and each handler are different, I cannot tell you what an assistance dog can do for you or what benefits you would receive. Instead, I will guide you through a thought process that you can use to better understand *where* within in your life and *how* an assistance dog can possibly help you.

As you read this section, take time to think critically about what skills would be most beneficial for an assistance dog to provide you. Remember, not every skill that an assistance dog can perform may be necessary for you. Additionally, you may think of skills that are not described below which could be helpful and trained. So, keep an open mind as you read on. Also, take time to discuss the benefits with family and friends in your support network, as they may have other ideas of ways an assistance dog could be beneficial to you.

🐾 Before reading the next sections, take a moment to write down the benefits you hope an assistance dog will provide you.

Physical benefits

The most well-understood type of benefit an assistance dog provides their handler is physical. These benefits arise from the physical tasks the dog is trained to perform to mitigate the handler's disability. This often includes retrieving items, telling the handler information, showing the handler things, or assisting with tasks.

It is imperative that the assistance dog can perform this skill *reliably*. It is not enough for an assistance dog to just perform a skill that mitigates the handler's disability.

If the dog can't or doesn't perform reliably, what use is that? If the dog only performs the skill on their terms—say, because they can't be bothered to get off the couch or stop playing outside—it gives no help to their handler, especially in an emergency. For the handler's safety and peace of mind, an assistance dog needs to be reliable across various environments and distractions.

An assistance dog needs to be reliable and prompt when bringing their handler requested items, also known as retrieves. This could be retrieving something the handler drops or a named object that stays in a specific place and the dog knows where to get it. For example, the handler fell and needs a phone to call for help. The dog needs to know which object (phone) the handler is referring to when saying, "Get phone."

Then the dog needs to know where that phone always lives (e.g., on the hall dresser) and be prompt in getting it, as the handler may be in pain or danger. If the handler drops an object—say, a wallet—while crossing the street, you want the dog to efficiently pick it up and not be too distracted by the cars or people around to do their job. If the assistance dog is not reliable in retrieving, this could put the handler, waiting in the street for the dog or a passer-by to assist, in danger.

For alert dogs especially, they need to be reliable in telling the handler about a change that they are trained to perceive. Maybe the handler is about to have a seizure, the fire alarm is sounding, or the handler's blood sugar is dropping dangerously fast. For the handler's safety, the dog must not only *identify* this information but also have the desire to pass it to their handler. Sharing this information requires training, as it is not something most dogs do naturally. This could be because they may lack the motivation, or perhaps they don't realize we don't smell or sense the same things as they do. Since not all dogs will care to tell us, it takes training to teach a dog that we want to know this information and make sure they are reliable in reporting it to their handler.

When a dog alerts a handler to some information, it's typically done through a paw touch or a nose nudge. In either case, the dog knows the gesture means, *"The information or change you want to know about is happening."* Then a handler needs to interpret the information. Do not blindly trust your dog's alerts. This is important because maybe the dog was alerting in hopes of getting a treat or to notify you that there is a squirrel outside. These are called false alerts and should be identified yet ignored to teach the dog that that's not the information you want. For diabetic handlers, for example, verifying your dog's alerts involves checking your blood sugar.

In addition to notifying you about the information you want to know, assistance dogs may also need to show you where something is located. This is especially relevant for hearing alert dogs because without the handler knowing which sound or where it came from, the alert to the sound is useless. Therefore, once notified that a sound is occurring, handlers often use another cue such as "show me," where the dog is trained to lead the handler to the source of the sound. Guide dogs also spend time showing their handler where certain places—e.g., stairs, doors, chairs, or counters—are.

Assistance dogs can also assist in performing tasks. In the case of laundry, for example, by taking clean clothes out of the dryer and putting them into a basket. They can also open doors or assist in other physical actions the handler may not be able to perform or do so only with great effort. To open a door, for example, a dog could push the access button outside a public place or tug on a rope attached to the door handle. There are many ways assistance dogs can physically assist a person.

Irrespective of the physical task, it will take a lot of training and reinforcement for a dog to perform such skills reliably. These skills, a dog doesn't usually know intuitively. Although there are exceptions, it typically takes encouragement to foster these skills so that a dog realizes when they are appropriate and when not. Most importantly, a dog needs to be dependable because, otherwise, the handler could be in serious danger.

What can a dog physically do for me?

Prospective assistance dog handlers commonly comment that they don't know everything an assistance dog can do for them. That is okay! It's probably partly why you are reading this book. Although I cannot go through every possible thing an assistance dog could physically do for each person, I can assist you in thinking about the skills you may need a dog to perform and go over the most common skills for each type of dog.

The best way to figure out the physical tasks a dog could provide you is to start by thinking about and then writing down the challenges you experience in daily life that limit you from living a full life. Think about which activities of daily living are challenging for you. What takes up a lot of time or energy when you do it by yourself? Or what do you commonly need help from another person to do? Your list may look something like this:

1. I drop a lot of items and I'm at risk of falling when I pick them up.
2. When I have low blood sugar, I struggle to get myself to the fridge to get juice.
3. It takes me forever to get the laundry out of the dryer because I can't bend down and reach into the machine without becoming off balance.

4. I have difficulty hearing my name being called, especially in a busy environment.

5. After a seizure, I am too weak to get a weighted blanket, but they help me recover from a seizure quicker.

6. My child disappears into random areas in the store, and I worry about losing her.

7. I have trouble navigating my environment on my own due to my vision loss.

8. I don't feel secure walking into my house when it's dark.

9. I commonly lose my phone because I can't hear it fall out of my pocket.

10. I don't feel comfortable eating out in public because I don't know if my allergen is present in the food I order.

🐾 Give it a try: Use the next page to write out any activities of daily living that are challenging, things that take too much time or energy, or things you commonly need help with.

Once you believe your list is complete, ask friends and family to verify it. You and your support system know your needs best. They may have additional suggestions of things you struggle with daily. Possibly, you don't realize it because it has become such a normal part of your life.

Your next step is to translate your list into ways an assistance dog might assist you. Remember, dogs are good at retrieving things, telling you things, showing you things, and helping you with things. However, they are limited in what they can do—limited by their physical size and strength, their dexterity and coordination, and their ability to communicate with us.

Taking these factors into consideration, we can translate the list of challenges affecting our daily living into what a dog could assist us with. From the previous list, this may translate to:

1. A dog could retrieve dropped items for me.
2. A dog could open the fridge and retrieve juice for me.
3. A dog could get items out of the dryer for me (as long as it is a front-loading dryer with a door that swings to the side and not down).
4. A dog could alert me that someone is calling my name.
5. A dog could retrieve the weighted blanket or act like the weighted blanket by lying on me.
6. A dog could be attached to my child with a tether and act as an anchor by not moving when my child bolts, thereby preventing her from disappearing.
7. A dog could guide me to the coffee shop.
8. A dog could turn on the lights for me before I enter my house.

9. A dog could alert me to a dropped phone or other objects.
10. A dog could alert me to the presence of my allergen.

Below is a (not comprehensive) list of the physical tasks each assistance dog type can be trained to perform:

- **Guide Dogs**: guide their handler around obstacles and through busy environments; find doors, counters, chairs, or benches; stop at curbs and stairs; and lead straight across a street so their handler doesn't veer into traffic.
- **Mobility Assistance Dogs**: retrieve dropped items, or named items such as a phone or cane; open doors/drawers; close doors/drawers; press push-plates/buttons on automatic doors; put clothes or other items into a basket; carry or drag a bag or basket; go get a person for help or push an emergency button; remove certain items of clothing (like shoes, socks, pants, jackets). Assist up from a fall and assist with forward momentum. For wheelchair users, a dog can adjust the footplate, also can tug a manual wheelchair or walker to the handler.
- **Diabetic Alert Dogs**: alert to high and/or low blood sugars; retrieve juice, snacks, or something that will assist the handler to regain a normal blood sugar level. Get help via a person or emergency button.
- **Seizure Response Dogs**: get help via a person or emergency button; retrieve rescue medications, a

pillow, or a blanket; perform reviving behaviors like licking or nudging specific areas of the body, such as the hands or face.

- **Seizure Alert Dogs**: alert to seizure plus the seizure response dog tasks.

- **Hearing Alert Dogs**: alert to timers, phone ringing, fire alarm, alarm clock, door knock, doorbell, name calls; alert to a dropped item, baby crying, or other important sounds.

- **Autism Assistance Dogs**: prevent elopement (wandering off or bolting), interrupt stimming behaviors, offer deep pressure therapy, and know tricks to increase social engagement.

- **Psychiatric Assistance Dogs**: turn on lights, interrupt nightmares, provide deep pressure therapy, get help via a person or emergency button, check a room before entering, provide physical space in public, and interrupt repetitive or harmful behaviors.

- **Medical Alert Dogs:** Alert you to signs or symptoms of your medical condition. Get help via a person or emergency button.

🐾 Give it a try: Use the next page to write out how you think an assistance dog could (or could not) help you with your list of challenges. Remember, some of the challenges you experience, an assistance dog will not be able to help you with; some they can.

When you look at your list, prioritize which skills are *most* important to you. Prioritization is important, as assistance dogs can learn many skills. Just because a dog *can* do something for you doesn't always mean that they *should*. For example, just because a dog can be trained to do guide work doesn't mean they *should* be trained for that if it's not a skill the handler needs. Assistance dogs should be trained to master the skills their handler currently needs or based on the expected progression of their disability is expected to need in the future. If you can do something for yourself easily and reliably, that's not something a dog needs to perform.

🐾 Put numbers next to each skill, indicating the importance to you. #1 will be most important, #2 second most important, continuing until all your skills are numbered.

Now it's time to think more deeply about whether these skills are realistic for a dog to perform. When considering if a skill is realistic, we need to consider a few things.

Is it physically something a dog can do?

Dogs don't have opposable thumbs, so *they can't open a door with a round doorknob*. There are physical limitations to what they can do. However, they can open a door if a lever door handle is properly adapted for them. Think about the physical size and stature of a dog. Dogs are only so tall and walk on all four feet, so as hard as they try, they can't reach the top shelf in your kitchen to bring you something. These are some examples of skills that because of a dog's physical nature are unrealistic to expect from a dog.

How much effort or energy will it take for a dog to perform?

Just like humans, dogs are constrained by size. They are only so big, with so much muscle and so much energy. For example, they may physically be able to pull you in your wheelchair (depending on your size, your dog's size, and your type and size of wheelchair), but is it fair for them to do this once? Repeatedly? When do you need assistance with your wheelchair? In going over curbs or up inclines? I believe, *pulling you in your wheelchair is not reasonable to ask of a dog.* Not only could it physically injure your dog, but it will also significantly shorten the working life of your dog.

How demanding will it be on the dog?

Ask yourself, *is this skill something I need only occasionally, or will my dog be doing it multiple times per day, every day?* For example, do you have seizures ten to twenty times per day, every day, including at night, and expect your dog to either alert you to them or respond to each of them? Will this prevent the dog from getting adequate sleep? Are you asking your dog to pull your laundry up two flights of stairs? Think about how physically demanding what you are asking will be. Dogs can do incredible things, but only if *appropriate* in relation to their physiology and the skills needed. Also, allow for rest time, as to be successful in their job, they need rest.

Could it injure or scare the dog?

If you want a dog to break your fall, think again. Even if you have a Great Dane or other giant breed and you are a very small person, even a child, I don't recommend relying on a dog to break your fall. This is not only incredibly physically taxing on the dog and will significantly shorten the working life due to the wear and tear on the body, it can also scare the dog. Their natural reaction is to move away from objects (including people) falling toward them. It is not fair or right to ask this of your assistance dog.

Is it easier for a person or technology to assist?

If you want an alert to remind you to take your meds every three hours, including in the middle of the night, you could set an alarm for every three hours and allow your dog to do other things for you instead. If you are hard of hearing and have no other way of waking up in the middle of the night to take your meds, then consider what you can relieve the dog of during the day, allowing it to be more alert at night.

Another example is alerting to storm sirens. These sirens are infrequent, and you don't have control over when they sound, so this alert could be difficult to train for. Instead, you could watch for a storm other ways. For example, look outside at the weather, download a severe-weather app onto your phone, or notice how other people are reacting to the weather. Although your dog could technically give this alert, is it worth it and reasonable to ask?

Will the training be dangerous?

Some things a dog could do, but the training may be exceptionally risky—more dangerous than having the skill is worth. For example, hearing alert dogs could alert you to sirens when you are driving; however, teaching this skill can be fraught with danger. First, it involves your dog getting your attention, shifting it away from the road or highway. Then you need to figure out what your dog is alerting to and make sure it's not a false alert, just to get a treat. Additionally, giving rewards while driving can be distracting. Finally, there are other ways to know sirens are around; for example, using your mirrors to watch for flashing lights. Or being observant of other cars pulling over. This skill is more dangerous to train for than it's worth, as there are other methods of getting this information.

Finally, are you asking too much of your dog?

If you have multiple disabilities—for example, are diabetic and have hearing loss and mobility challenges—be cautious that you are not asking too much of your assistance dog. This is especially important for alert dogs, who can feel like they are always on the job because they never know when an alert may be needed. Decide which skills would benefit you the most, rather than asking your dog to do *everything* it is physically capable of. Your dog will thank you.

🐾 Now that you have a better idea of what is not reasonable to ask of a dog, go back to your list of skills that you developed earlier in this chapter and cross out any you now think are unrealistic. Draw a question mark next to the ones you are unsure of and will ask a professional about.

It is important to share your list with a professional in the assistance dog industry to get feedback and set realistic expectations. If you do not have realistic expectations, you will be disappointed in the dog's abilities, your relationship will be strained, and overall you will be more likely to not form a mutually beneficial relationship or be successful. Therefore, take time to carefully think through what you want an assistance dog to physically do for you and get assistance from a professional if needed. Chapter 13 will discuss how to choose a professional in the field to work with.

Benefits from physical skills

The trained physical skills an assistance dog performs provide considerable benefit to their handler. Closely associated with the dog's physical skills, other benefits commonly arise, such as decreased assistance needed from another person and the ability to save energy.

In some instances, an assistance dog can provide skills that other people, such as a Personal Care Assistant (PCA), commonly perform. Whether or not your assistance dog can minimize the need for this type of assistance will depend on your level of need, the things your PCA does, and the degree of overlap in what your dog is trained to do. Sometimes assistance dogs can help reduce the number of PCA hours needed, sometimes not. Most likely, an assistance dog will not replace a PCA.

Assistance dogs can also help prevent a handler from doing repetitive tasks that consume energy, such as repeatedly bending to pick up dropped items. Even though this skill may seem small, people often don't realize how much energy doing these things themselves is taking from them. When handlers, like Jane, are no longer chasing around the items they drop, they have more energy to do other things that they had previously given up on because they were too tired, like cooking dinner.

These are typically the most common benefits that people think of in reference to assistance dogs. However, you need to think carefully about what skills you want an assistance dog to do for you—what would be most beneficial—and whether these are realistic for a dog to perform. The trained benefits also impact the untrained benefits.

🐾 What benefits and challenges can you add to your pros and cons list?

CHAPTER 3

Untrained benefits

Untrained benefits are either a byproduct of the trained benefits or arise naturally from the relationship of working with a dog. The untrained benefits are most commonly described as psychological or social benefits.

Psychological benefits

Psychological benefits provided by an assistance dog involve increased feelings of safety or security, independence, confidence, feelings of companionship, and consequently decreased depression or anxiety. These benefits arise from the physical tasks an assistance dog performs, the physical presence of the dog, or even the placebo effect. Irrespective of how the benefits arise, the psychological benefits of an assistance dog are incredibly important to the overall well-being of the handler.

Safety

Assistance dogs are commonly reported to help their handler feel safer or more secure. Each type of assistance dog can provide safety or feelings of safety in their own way. For example:

- **Guide Dogs** help their handler safely cross the street or guide them around obstacles that they could otherwise run into.
- **Mobility Assistance Dogs** can retrieve a dropped cane or a walker that rolled away from them or assist them up from a fall.
- **Diabetic Alert Dogs** alert to changes in blood sugar before it becomes life-threatening.
- **Seizure Alert Dogs** alert to seizures so the handler can get to a safe place where they are less likely to fall or hurt themselves.
- **Seizure Response Dogs** get help for the handler when a seizure is occurring or just after.
- **Hearing Alert Dogs** notify the handler of the fire alarm or other life-saving sounds.
- **Autism Assistance Dogs** help keep the child safe by preventing elopement in public.
- **Psychiatric Assistance Dogs** help with feeling safe by having a dog check the room for them or turn on lights before entering.
- **Medical Alert Dogs** alert to a spike in their handler's medical condition or alert to an allergen in the environment so the handler can take action before it becomes life-threatening.

Beyond the skills that can provide physical safety, any type of assistance dog can be trained in the three common ways to "get help." First, by bringing a designated phone to their handler, who can then call for help. Second, the dog can press an emergency button that automatically contacts family, friends, or emergency services. Third, they can get an adult within the home who will follow the assistance dog back to the handler to provide aid. All three ways of getting help increase the handler's safety.

When dogs are getting help, they are typically in their home environment; this is where it's safest for the dog to perform this skill. It can be unsafe to have a dog get help in public because when on a leash, they can only go so far. If you drop the leash, you have no control over who your dog goes to or how far to get help. There is also no guarantee they will come back. You may think: *But my dog loves me. He will come back*. Take a moment to think like a dog. If you are unresponsive, your dog will probably be stressed, and since you can't reward them for coming back, they may relieve their stress by getting away. If you need help in public, typically the physical presence of your dog in a cape, being identified as an assistance dog, is enough for someone to come over and offer help.

Many people report increased feelings of safety in public, even if their dog lacks the trained ability to get help. This is especially true for handlers of alert dogs. Alerts allow the handler to feel safe doing things outside of the home, counting on the advance notice of an alert to get to a safe place or be able to take care of themselves before a dangerous situation arises.

It is important to note that assistance dogs are not in any way protection dogs and should not be used as such. Even psychiatric assistance dogs, often perceived to "have their handler's back" (or got their six), do not, and should not, provide protection work. An assistance dog should never be trained to attack someone who gets too close or who gives signs of intending to hurt the handler. In the example where a psychiatric assistance dog has the handler's back, the dog is simply facing the other direction, and by reading the dog's body language, the handler may pick up on the fact that someone is approaching.

This is similar to people who are Deaf or hard of hearing. These dogs typically don't alert to the presence of people behind them, but by looking at their dog's body language and noticing when the dog looks back, the handler can recognize the presence of someone in back. Therefore, it's the psychological feeling of safety—of being watched out for—that is most beneficial, rather than the dog doing anything other than facing the other direction or naturally moving their head.

You may have noticed that a side effect of a lot of the dog's skills involves providing *a feeling of safety* rather than providing physical safety. This is because an assistance dog is a dog and is imperfect. They will make mistakes—miss alerts or not respond to commands—potentially when you need them the most. Therefore, it is possible that the dog will not do their job when you most need them to. For example, no alert dog is guaranteed to alert 100 percent of the time. They are not a robot, after all. However, handlers feel safe, knowing that their dog can do these things for them and trusting that the dog will when needed.

Therefore, realistic expectations are important because 100 percent reliance on your dog is unrealistic and can provide a false sense of safety. This overreliance can put the handler in more danger if not taking normal precautions. Irrespective of how the dog provides a feeling of safety, this benefit does increase the handler's quality of life and well-being.

Independence

Another psychological benefit that assistance dogs provide is independence. This typically arises in two ways.

First, as most prominently seen with guide dogs and mobility assistance dogs, the physical skills provided allow the handler to be more independent. Both types of dogs use their physical skills to help the handler be independent in ways they could not be without a dog. For example, guide dogs help their handler get to work independently, and mobility dogs help their handler retrieve things or open doors, not having to wait for a passer-by or rely on friends or family to assist.

The second way an assistance dog can provide independence is through the psychological feeling of safety, allowing the handler to feel comfortable going in public independently. For example, in the case of alert dogs, believing they will be alerted so they can take care of themselves. This feeling of safety also applies to psychiatric assistance dogs, whose handlers commonly don't feel comfortable going in public alone. Both allow the handler to be more independent.

Assistance dogs do not provide an increase in independence equally to every handler. Nor do they typically enable complete independence. For many people, it is unrealistic to expect total independence with an assistance dog when they were far from independent initially. The degree of independence a handler can gain by working with an assistance dog is relative to the handler's disability, age, and cognitive ability.

The independence gained needs to be age appropriate. For example, it is not reasonable to expect a child handler to become independent just by having an assistance dog. However, children handlers may be able to regain independence similar to that of their peers or become independent at home. Also, depending on the severity of the disability or cognitive ability of the handler, independence may be variable.

Independence is an incredible benefit of having an assistance dog, as it can provide access to a life that the handler may have never had access to explore before. This is incredibly important to handlers and often provides other subsequent benefits, such as increasing their confidence and overall well-being.

Confidence

Working with an assistance dog can dramatically increase a person's confidence, irrespective of having a congenital or acquired disability. People with congenital disabilities working with an assistance dog often gain confidence in themselves in doing things independently that they never thought possible before. This could be going in public by themselves or even moving out of the home. People with acquired disabilities, especially those who rapidly lost their ability to do things or care for themselves, can also gain a great deal of confidence that the disability took from them.

For both populations, increasing confidence can lead to great strides in other areas of their life. No matter where this confidence comes from, whether it be the training and working with a dog, the newfound independence, the feeling of safety, etc., the increase in confidence is incredibly important to bolstering their self-worth, self-esteem, and overall quality of life. When people feel confident in themselves, they can do great things.

Companionship

Beyond the physical tasks an assistance dog can do, the physical presence of their dog can also provide psychological benefits—known as companionship.

Companionship from a dog is especially beneficial because it fosters feelings of unconditional acceptance. It is generally believed that dogs love and accept you unconditionally. They accept you as you are and do not judge. Their unconditional love is just the ticket that some people need to have confidence in themselves, feel good about themselves, feel less lonely, and increase their feelings of well-being. This can also help to decrease depression or anxiety.

Dogs in general are great at providing companionship to their person just by being around. This is not unique to assistance dogs and is not a *skill* that an assistance dog learns (although commonly incorrectly reported as a skill). This is because dogs provide companionship without training. Any dog can do this. Therefore, companionship is a beneficial byproduct of working with a dog.

Consequently, if you listed companionship as a skill that you want your dog to provide, remove it from your list. If this was the only skill you wrote down for an assistance dog to provide (including emotional support), then what you really want is an emotional support animal. Lucky for you, they are much easier to acquire and provide great emotional support and companionship within the home.

Additionally, companionship is an incredibly important benefit for people who may be socially isolated or have become socially isolated because of their disability. An assistance dog can help their handler feel less alone. Not only can their dog be with them at home and accompany them in public, but dogs are also a great social catalyst, as discussed next.

🐾 How do you feel your dog will increase your feelings of safety? Is it directly related to the physical task it can perform, or do you expect a psychological benefit?

🐾 In what ways will your assistance dog NOT increase your independence? In what ways will they increase your independence?

Social benefits

Similar to companionship benefits, dogs are naturals at providing social benefits!

This benefit arises from the "social catalyst effect" in that— at least the Western world—people, in general, like dogs, are attracted to dogs, want to chat with you about your dog or chat with you because you have a dog with you. Although anyone with a dog can experience the social catalyst effect, it can be more pronounced for assistance dog handlers. This is because seeing an assistance dog in public is more common than seeing a companion dog and because assistance dogs typically go where companion dogs are not allowed. This unique quality of assistance dogs attracts a lot of attention to handlers.

The attention handlers receive in this way is generally positive; mostly, handlers find the benefits of the social catalyst effect, like making friends and having friendly conversations with the public about their dog, enjoyable. However, handlers often underestimate the power of the social catalyst effect—that is, how frequently people will stop you in public to chat about your assistance dog.

Through these interactions, assistance dogs reportedly help their handler make friends and form relationships in their community, as they are easily recognized. These offhand conversations, often with strangers, are typically positive, casual exchanges about the assistance dog; however, the public can be judgmental or critical as well.

It is very usual for handlers to be approached in public to talk about their dog. This positive social interaction is often a welcome change if you have a visible disability because, it is commonly reported, the usual response of avoiding eye contact or, in any case, not striking up a conversation doesn't occur. When you go in public with an assistance dog, this changes. Often people make eye contact and smile at handlers. Also, they want to interact because of the dog.

Another perhaps-unforeseen consequence of having an assistance dog in public is how conspicuous you become. If you do not have a visible disability, you may not have previously had negative experiences in public resulting from a visible disability. However, working with an assistance dog, you will no longer be invisible, which brings its own challenges. You will now be labeled as having a disability. But as you have an assistance dog, this is seen in a more positive light. As illustrated in the situation below, however, it can seem like too much.

An assistance dog, Max, was trained by an assistance dog organization, who then transitioned Max over to a first-time handler, Joe. Together they had been working for a week with the organization's trainer. The training took place in and around the community the organization resided in. Once Max got home, Joe became overwhelmed by the constant requests in public to pet Max or chat with him while he was running errands. After the first couple of weeks, the overwhelmed handler realized the assistance dog would continue to attract attention for the rest of their working life. Joe decided the extra attention was impossible for him to adapt to, that it slowed down his ability to run errands, and unfortunately returned Max to the organization. The extra unwanted attention when they went home was most likely due to the limited familiarity

Joe's local community had with assistance dogs, compared to the community around the assistance dog organization.

Joe's story demonstrates that handlers need to expect that an assistance dog will draw attention to them in public and attract people who want to stop and chat, no matter whether they are in a hurry or not. Potentially a lot. If you want more social interaction, this is a great way to build friendships and positive relationships. However, the dog can only do so much in that regard. After all, the assistance dog can't invite anyone to join you for coffee; only you, the handler, can do that.

Overall, assistance dogs can provide many benefits for the handler that are not a specific part of their training. These benefits often arise from the physical skills or tasks an assistance dog is trained to do; however, they can also arise from the *mere presence* of the dog. These untrained benefits include feelings of safety, independence, confidence, companionship, and having more positive social experiences. Together, these also help to increase a handler's quality of life and well-being.

🐾 If increasing social interaction and making friends is something that you want your assistance dog to facilitate, how do you plan to foster these social interactions into friendships?

🐾 What other benefits besides physical skills are you looking forward to an assistance dog providing you?

🐾 What benefits and challenges can you add to your pros and cons list?

Takeaways

Based on the information presented in Part 1, you should be able to differentiate between assistance dogs, emotional support animals, and therapy dogs. You should have a better understanding of what types of assistance dogs are out there and whom they help. Additionally, you should have a better understanding of what they could possibly do to help mitigate your disability through specific skills they can be trained to perform, the subsequent benefits or the benefit that dogs in general can provide.

Based on the information presented in Part 1, do you believe an assistance dog can assist with your disability?

🐾 Why or why won't they assist you with your disability?

Part 1 Learning Objectives

After reading this section you should be able to...

- differentiate between commonly used terminology.
- identify the eight types of assistance dogs based on the common disabilities they assist with.
- describe why an assistance dog is, in this framework, a piece of medical equipment.
- list common physical skills that each type of assistance dog can perform.
- recognize realistic and unrealistic expectations regarding physical skills for an assistance dog.
- describe the psychological and social benefits and how they arise.

Part 2

Can you create a mutually beneficial partnership with a dog?

The purpose of having an assistance dog is for the dog to mitigate some effects of your disability. Dogs can't do this, however, if not properly cared for. Assistance dogs need to be healthy and thriving to help you be healthy and thriving. This describes a mutually beneficial relationship.

Adding an assistance dog into your life must create a mutually beneficial partnership. Otherwise, the relationship will be unbalanced, and one being will receive more benefit while the other has more burden. To prevent this lack of balance, it is highly important that you know—before you add an assistance dog into your life—whether you can foster a mutually beneficial relationship. The nuances to forming a mutually beneficial relationship will be discussed throughout this section.

Assistance dogs are first and foremost dogs. As such, they take a lot of time, energy, and work compared to the maintenance of other assistive devices. They are not robots. They cannot be unplugged or put in a closet at the end of the day. You can't just take them out when it's convenient for you and the rest of the time ignore them. They need a lot of your time and attention. They also need food, water, shelter, exercise, rest, enrichment, medical care, and more.

In this section I will describe aspects of their care and your life that will contribute to or detract from your ability to create a mutually beneficial relationship with an assistance dog. First, as you read, reflect on whether you can fully care for the dog physically, mentally, emotionally, and financially. If the relationship is going to work, it is imperative that you provide for and meet all the dog's daily needs. If you are unable to meet any of your dog's basic needs, the dog won't be able to assist you, as their needs *must* be met first.

Then we will discuss lifestyle considerations, including personal factors, other members of your household, your housing situation, and your work or school considerations. Each of these factors can contribute to your ability to work successfully with an assistance dog and are important to consider before starting this journey.

By reading this section, you will learn what areas of your life you may need to change before welcoming an assistance dog into your life. Even if your lifestyle is not suitable now, in the future it could be.

This section will also discuss options for how to create a mutually beneficial relationship even if you can't fully care for the assistance dog independently all the time. If you yourself, alone, can't meet the dog's needs, you must put a plan in place with your support network that will assist you with whatever aspect of their care you are unable to provide. If you, with your support network, are still unable to properly care for a dog, then an assistance dog is not an appropriate tool to assist you with your disability, and ethically, you should not get one.

This section will help you determine the answer to the above question.

Part 2 learning objectives

By the end of reading Part 2, you will be able to…

- determine if you can care for an assistance dog physically, mentally, and emotionally.
- determine if you can financially afford an assistance dog.
- determine if your lifestyle is appropriate for utilizing an assistance dog.
- determine if other members of your home will be okay with the addition of an assistance dog.
- prepare your home so it is suitable for an assistance dog.
- prepare to talk with your employer or school about having an assistance dog.

CHAPTER 4

Physical care

Physically caring for an assistance dog allows the dog to care for you physically too. This means providing them with proper nutrition and exercise appropriate to their size, age, and energy level—consistently and appropriately. If not, your assistance dog will struggle to do their job.

Nutrition

To properly care for an assistance dog, you need the ability to provide high-quality food and clean water consistently. Assistance dogs deserve the best nutrition possible. After all, they need sustenance to assist you. High-quality food in an appropriate amount will keep your dog healthier, and therefore able to work for longer.

Consistent high-quality food is important because switching diets frequently is not good for the dog's overall health and could cause stomach upset. An upset stomach is not only hard on your dog but also hard on you, as the dog shouldn't work, probably won't want to work, and if it does work, especially in public, it could result in an unexpected accident.

Providing high-quality food, while important, can be more expensive than lower-quality food. Therefore, be sure you can financially afford to consistently provide a dog with high-quality food. It is not appropriate if, for example, you need to switch food, depending on what type is on sale. If this is your strategy, you are unable to properly care for an assistance dog, and until you can financially afford good-quality dog food on a consistent basis, you should reconsider it as a tool for you. Alternatively, determine how you can alter your budget to financially accommodate your dog's food (and other) needs.

Beyond consideration for what type of food you provide, you also need to be committed to providing the proper *amount* of food to keep your dog in peak physical performance. These are working dogs. They should maintain a body condition where the dog has a waist when viewed from above, has an abdominal tuck when viewed from the side, and you can easily feel their ribs. An assistance dog should be neither too thin nor overweight, as either direction will impact their ability to work for you. You need to commit now to maintaining a healthy dog.

An overweight assistance dog is not only unhealthy, but excess pounds add unnecessary strain on the body and they can decrease the dog's life by a couple of years. This is especially important to consider for dogs who may already have added strain on their joints due to the type of work they do, such as wearing a harness for guide or mobility work, dogs who do bracing, or dogs who pull or carry larger items.

As an assistance dog handler, it is your responsibility to keep the dog's best interests in mind and be proactive in caring for them. As dogs can be very good at hiding pain and soreness, it's up to you to seek out resources to assist your dog before it's too late, especially if in the case of doing physically demanding work. Be prepared financially to take your dog to a canine chiropractor or masseuse to keep their joints and muscles ready for work. This extra care can significantly increase the length of your dog's working life, so take it seriously.

It is important to think about how you will deal with these challenges now, rather than struggle to properly care for a dog once you have them. Use the space below to create a plan.

🐾 What do you plan to do if your finances change?

🐾 What do you plan to do if your dog starts becoming overweight?

✿ Think about previous dogs you have owned: were you able to maintain them at an appropriate body condition throughout their life?

Exercise

Maintaining proper nutrition and weight and providing sufficient exercise is incredibly important for an assistance dog. Here's a cautionary story that happens too often. Katie got a fully grown assistance dog, named Rufus, from an assistance dog organization. Within a year, the dog had gained an additional 25 percent above the veterinarian-determined "ideal" body weight for Rufus. This was due to Katie's inability to exercise Rufus as much as she'd expected to before getting him.

As her disability progressed and given the harsh nature of the winter climate Katie lived in, she encountered extra challenges in providing enough exercise for the dog initially. Struggling under the added weight, Rufus found it difficult to do normal dog things like jump into a vehicle. Due to Katie's inability to sufficiently exercise and care for Rufus, this is not a mutually beneficial relationship.

The typical work an assistance dog performs is not considered exercise. Beyond this, dogs need an energy outlet. They are active animals. As I said before, assistance dogs can't be put in a closet and forgotten about when you aren't using them. If not given a sufficient energy outlet proactively, they can and will create their own by tearing up the home or engaging in other destructive activities. Not only can this ruin your personal property, it can also put the dogs in danger; for instance, suppose they ingest something they shouldn't or hurt themselves by not having a proper energy outlet.

This underscores how important it is that you provide your dog with suitable exercise. Without this, there cannot be a mutually beneficial relationship. Exercise typically takes the form of play, walks, games, enrichment, dog-dog play, etc. The best part is dogs love to exercise and will love engaging with you in this way. Compared to people, who often find exercising a chore, dogs seek it out. It's a great way to bond and strengthen your relationship. On the other hand, if you don't provide the dog with exercise, it can strain your relationship, the dog can gain weight, and all in all, it's not beneficial for either of you.

Many first-time handlers, especially if never having lived with an assistance dog (or companion dog) before, initially underestimate the amount of energy their assistance dog will have and therefore need to expend daily. This misconception arises because the assistance dogs they have seen in public are well-behaved and calm. To be calm in public, dogs need to have an appropriate energy outlet elsewhere during their day. Assistance dogs are not robots; they need downtime to play and have fun. That calmness in public takes practice and is *not* what an assistance dog is always like.

Initially, an assistance dog will be young and full of energy. Their energy outlet requirements will be higher than older dogs. Young dogs do not lounge around most of the day like some older dogs. Therefore, you need to be prepared to provide sufficient energy release for a young dog such as running and playing. Additionally, different breeds have different energy needs. Do your research on the energy level of the type of dog you may get.

For people who have never lived with a dog before or haven't in a while, seriously consider where you plan to sufficiently exercise your dog. This is incredibly important to think about now, before you have a dog at home and belatedly realize you can't exercise them properly. Think about your home. Where can you exercise a dog within your home? What room(s) have sufficient space? Do you have a long hallway you can use?

🐾 Describe where in your home you will exercise a dog. Be specific.

Where outside of your home can you exercise a dog? This may include your yard, neighborhood, local parks, etc. If you don't know or don't have much dog experience, ask your dog-owning family, friends, and neighbors where they exercise their dogs locally. If you don't already know, look for a local trail you can walk on. Is there one? Is it paved? Are the streets or sidewalks around your home safe for walking (think about all times of day and weather conditions)? Is there a local fenced-in tennis court you could use? How about accessibility? Are these places accessible with your equipment?

🐾 Describe where you will exercise a dog outside of your home. Be specific.

Once you know the locations, be aware that each dog enjoys a particular play style, so consider your ability to fetch, tug, chase, etc. Ensure that you are physically able to provide exercise, such as walking and playing. It is best to plan to engage with more than one play style, as dogs enjoy variety in play. When considering the types of play, realistically consider your abilities to engage with them in each action. Are you able to throw a ball repeatedly? Can you safely play tug or chase? Do you (or friends/family) have another dog-friendly dog for your dog to play with? Dogs appreciate variety in exercise, so make sure you have more than one exercise option available to you.

🐾 Describe what types of play you can physically do with your dog. Be specific.

You don't need to provide every type of play you can think of. However, they do enjoy it when play is varied so they don't get bored, repeating the same play or exercise routine every day. Additionally, not all dogs like fetch, so don't plan on fetch being the only way you exercise your dog. Don't worry if you're not an able-bodied athlete; dogs are good at adapting to your ability. Overall, play is an important way to bond, as, believe it or not, dogs enjoy it when you take an interest in what they enjoy.

However, be realistic. Consider what is feasible for you. Not what is aspirational. Not what you will magically be able to do just because you have an assistance dog.

Many prospective handlers say they will take their dog on a thirty-minute (or more) walk around the neighborhood daily. However, they don't or are unable to do this currently—maybe due to a lack of stamina, physical ability, or motivation.

If you currently lack the stamina or physical ability to walk for thirty minutes, an assistance dog won't change this fact. Rather, work to *build your stamina and strength now* so you can walk for thirty minutes with a dog once you have it. This practice will also help you to make sure it's part of your routine and will be continued with a dog.

Other factors to consider include determining whether your walking ability is sufficient for exercise. Is your walking pace fast enough? Are you able to walk far enough to get your dog exercised? Are you stable enough on your feet to safely walk them? A slow walk to the end of the street and back is not sufficient exercise for a young, healthy dog. If you don't believe you can walk fast enough, long enough, or are stable enough to walk a dog, consider whether other adaptive equipment can assist you to meet these needs, such as a power chair or scooter.

🐾 What qualities of your walking ability do you have that demonstrate you can safely and sufficiently walk a dog enough for them to get exercise?

If you currently lack the motivation to walk thirty minutes daily and think an assistance dog will magically help you gain motivation, you may be right, but you may also be wrong. Many people, like Katie with Rufus, promise themselves that *if* they have an assistance dog, they will be motivated to do a lot of things, *including walking more*. This doesn't always happen, as old routines and habits take precedence or because being tired from working with an assistance dog in other ways, you don't have the energy to go for a walk.

Therefore, start the walking routine now, before you get a dog. It is also good to practice your walking route now, so you know how to prepare for exercising your dog *in all seasons or weather conditions*. Does this route get too icy in the winter or flooded in the spring? Where will you go during these times instead?

A lot of assistance dog handlers face challenges providing their dog with enough exercise when the weather is not ideal. What will you do if the temperature is too hot, too cold, it's stormy or too icy/snowy? You know what the weather is like where you live, so plan for this now. If you know your wheelchair won't be able to utilize sidewalks during a snowy winter or it will be too icy for you to safely walk outside, consider how you can get yourself someplace inside where you can walk or provide other forms of exercise. Make sure to think outside the box!

Remember that assistance dogs have the privilege of being able to go for exercise walks *in a mall or other public spaces, where companion dogs are not allowed.* These locations can be great places for a walk inside on days when the weather is not great outside.

🐾 Which weather conditions (or other factors) will limit your ability to exercise a dog?

🐾 What ways can you exercise a dog during these times?

🐾 Where inside will you go to exercise a dog? Be specific.

The last thing you need to consider is time. Do you have enough time to exercise a dog? *Exercise should be a daily occurrence*, not reserved only for days you don't go out in public. Make sure you can dedicate thirty minutes minimum per day to exercising your dog. This doesn't need to be in one chunk, but at a minimum set aside thirty minutes to dedicate to your dog's exercise needs. Is this realistic for you? What will you do if your schedule gets busy?

It will be important to prioritize a dog's exercise needs over a busy schedule, or the dog won't be able to work for you. Carve out time in your schedule now to exercise a dog so business is not an excuse. The location, the types of exercise, and the time that you can exercise your dog are all important considerations before you get an assistance dog. Use the space below to plan for how you will overcome these challenges.

🐾 When during each day can I exercise my dog (e.g., before work, after dinner, from 2:00 to 3:00 p.m., etc.)?

- Sunday

- Monday

- Tuesday

- Wednesday

- Thursday

- Friday

- Saturday

🐾 What barriers do you see preventing you from exercising your dog daily?

🐾 How can you minimize these barriers?

The barriers you envision are especially important to consider now so you can have a plan in place to minimize them. Common barriers include having days where you have extremely low energy, high pain, or are mentally or physically having a bad day. For some people, their bad days are so bad they can't get out of bed. Consider how often these barriers occur for you and how limiting they are. If they are frequent and it will prevent you from being able to exercise or even engage with your dog successfully, an assistance dog might not be the right tool for you.

Although possible, it is not recommended to have another person exercise your dog on your bad days unless absolutely necessary. Beyond the fact that it is your dog, and it is your responsibility to meet their needs, exercise should be fun—something that the dog looks forward to. Exercise is a time for you to bond and spend time together, doing something the dog enjoys. If another person usurps this role regularly, your dog may start to feel like all you care about is work. This will put a strain on your relationship, as the dog will want to spend the most time with the fun person and may stop wanting to work for you or even be around you. This is extreme but possible if you are not the one meeting their exercise (aka fun) needs.

It is also not recommended to exercise your dog at a dog park. I strongly make this recommendation for several reasons. First, dog parks can make your dog sick. The water bowls or other shared spaces are rarely cleaned, and therefore bacteria can grow and pass along many illnesses to your dog. Through close proximity, dogs could also give your dog kennel cough or other contagious illnesses. Second, you do not know the behavior or temperament of the other dogs that are there. Finally, you do not know how well other owners can read their dog's body language and know if their dog is just playing or about to start a fight.

Fights and injuries are common at dog parks because of these unknowns. Are you physically able to break up a dog fight if your dog is involved? Additionally, it is important for handlers, more than companion dog owners, to make sure that their dog does not get injured at a dog park (or ever). An injury will make them unable to work for you while recovering. Depending on the severity of the injury or psychological implications on you or the dog, they may never be able to work again. Overall, dog parks provide more risk than reward, especially for a working assistance dog.

🐾 Based on your responses to the above questions, do you believe you can physically care for an assistance dog in a way that will meet their needs?

🐾 What benefits and challenges can you add to your pros and cons list?

CHAPTER 5

Mental and emotional care

Beyond physical care, you also need to care for a dog's mental and emotional health and well-being. This involves providing sufficient mental stimulation and rest. Additionally, you need to learn to read your dog's body language, especially stress signals, so you can assist them through stressful situations.

Mental stimulation

Assistance dogs need a lot of mental stimulation because they like to work and like to do things. From the tasks they are trained to do, they often get more mental stimulation than companion dogs. Frequently, this can lead to their "mental stimulation muscle" being stronger than in the case of other dogs—therefore, needing more mental stimulation to feel satisfied.

Mental stimulation can be influenced by the amount of, or mental difficulty of, the work they perform. Based on the handler's needs, assistance dogs may have variable amounts of work, depending on what the handler is doing that particular day or the handler's condition that day. In times when you require less from your dog, whether that's because you are feeling good and can do things yourself, or days that you are stuck at home and consequently doing less, it will be important to provide added mental stimulation for your dog, so they don't get bored and potentially destructive. They are dogs, after all.

One of the easiest ways to add mental activity for your dog is by setting up training sessions. Even if you don't need your dog's skills *that* day, by reinforcing them, you can keep them sharp. This is called maintenance training, and every assistance dog, no matter how well trained initially, will need it for life. Maintenance training involves practicing the skills your dog already knows and making sure you are reinforcing them with treats, play, or praise when your dog does a good job. They will enjoy these training sessions, and the maintenance training will help you keep your dog's skills in peak performance long-term.

Providing maintenance training is required for life. If you do not think you will realistically be able to provide maintenance training for your dog regularly, you will struggle as a team. Two common rules in dog training, more broadly than just the assistance dog world, are (1) if you don't use it, you will lose it, and (2) if you don't reinforce it, you will lose it. Both are incredibly important. Again, assistance dogs are dogs, not robots, so they will need reminders and continued training for life.

Another good way to provide mental stimulation for a dog is through enrichment. There are many forms of enrichment, and these are especially beneficial when you are not feeling well and can't do maintenance training, as these are things you can typically monitor your dog with rather than needing to interact. Enrichment is typically provided by using toys, including puzzle toys, or games that mimic natural dog behaviors like sniffing or foraging for food. Often, these involve hiding treats or food and making the dog work physically or mentally to access them. Simply providing a treat is not enrichment.

Often, enrichment items can be bought from a store, or they can be made with things around your house, like a towel. There are many resources available on making and providing enrichment activities for your dog. Therefore, research and determine what is feasible for you to do with the resources and budget you have.

For example, one way to provide the same enrichment goal of simulating foraging for food can be accomplished with a store-bought item (snuffle mat) or handy items around the house (towel or blanket). For either of these, you place your dog's food on it. With the towel/blanket you can bunch or wrap it up. With the snuffle mat you can poke the food into the mat. Either way, the dog has to work to get the food. Both are great ways to keep your dog mentally active and engaged.

🐾 How do you plan to provide mental stimulation on days when you are not feeling well?

🐾 What are some simple ways that you can help your dog be mentally active?

The dog will need rest to prevent burnout

On the opposite end of the spectrum from keeping the dog mentally active, your assistance dog will also need time to rest. You should not expect an assistance dog to be available to work for you 100 percent of the time 24/7. This is unrealistic. Just like humans need a weekend off from work, so will an assistance dog. If you are unwilling to let an assistance dog out of your sight or feel they need to be with you 24/7, then an assistance dog is not the right tool for you, as this is not healthy for them.

Your dog's "weekend" will probably look different from the standard working person's weekend. Where assistance dogs may not take two full days off work in a row (although they may love that), they should ideally have one rest day per week and daily rest time away from the handler.

This rest time should occur proactively in a designated space that the dog can go to and feel safe. Commonly, this involves a kennel, or crate. Retiring to this designated space or being put there, the dog should feel comfortable and relaxed, knowing you won't ask them to do any work. Here, they can rest, recover, and be reenergized for their next time working.

Designated rest time away from the handler is incredibly important because this is when the dog can truly sleep. You may think an assistance dog lying at the handler's feet in a restaurant, for example, is sleeping. Perhaps this is so. However, as soon as the handler drops a spoon, the dog will wake up and happily retrieve it. Or the dog may be sleeping at the handler's feet while watching TV but wakes up upon noticing a change in the handler's blood sugar level. In both situations, the dog is not *fully* sleeping, as the sleep can be disrupted to do their job. Therefore, the dog needs to have down time to sleep, knowing it's a disturbance-free, interruption-free period.

As some assistance dogs perform very demanding, time-consuming skills, this rest period is incredibly important. For example, alert dogs may be constantly vigilant to detect changes in blood sugar levels, an oncoming seizure, or important sounds or allergens in the environment. Constant vigilance is exhausting, especially if they are expected to work at night, when their handler is sleeping, as well as during the day. It is extra important that these dogs receive time off where they are not responsible for your condition or safety.

During the time a dog is off duty, another person should be around, someone you've entrusted to assist you. If you don't have another person able to assist you, another good time to allow your dog to rest is when you feel you are in a good place with your condition or are trusting other equipment so your dog can truly rest.

Certain dogs' skills are more *physically* demanding. For example, performing tasks such as guiding you around obstacles, pulling laundry baskets, retrieving things at a distance, or bracing can be physically demanding. These can make a dog physically tired, especially if repeated multiple times in a row or multiple times throughout the day. Therefore, the dog needs a time when they know nothing will be asked of them.

To prevent burnout, for all types of assistance dogs, rest is incredibly important. Just like people need time off from their job, so do assistance dogs. If you don't give them this time off proactively, they will learn to take it when they want it, which could occur at an inopportune time for you. Or they may get burnt out and stop doing their job altogether. It is your responsibility as the handler to make sure you are not overworking your dog and that you, rather, are keeping their best interests in mind, including designated rest every day. If not, you will not form a mutually beneficial partnership.

🐾 Where will you allow your dog to rest when you won't ask anything of them?

🐾 Who or what will assist you while your dog is resting?

Assisting them through stressful situations

Beyond providing mental stimulation and rest, another way that you need to care for your dog is by recognizing when it is stressed and, if so, being able to help the dog through such situations. Therefore, you will need to be observant of your dog's body language, as this is a dog's primary form of communication.

Just as you don't like being stressed, neither does your dog. Therefore, it is important that you know how to identify your dog's stress indicators so you can reduce or eliminate the stressor. This is not a skill you need to be great at initially, as it will be learned while working with a dog, but it is important that you can be observant to your dog's subtle body language changes.

Are you an observant person? If so, you will do better at this. If not, practice. If you have a dog or access to dogs, practice noticing what they notice and identifying the shift in body language when they become stressed or distracted. Both are important for you to identify to help your dog work successfully.

Common signals for distraction involve their gaze changing focus or intensity, their ears changing position to be more forward when they are curious or backward when they are scared. Their tail may stop (or start) wagging, or their body posture and how they hold their weight can also shift, depending on how they feel about the distraction. These subtle body cues and changes are how your dog communicates with you. You must be able to identify and accurately interpret these behaviors so you can notice what your dog is distracted by, as they can't work when they are distracted.

Additionally, you need the ability to identify common stress behaviors, which might look like normal dog behaviors but out of context. This includes scratching when they are not itchy. Yawning when they are not tired. Panting when it's not hot out. Lip licking when they are not getting the crumbs off their mouth or anticipating a treat. Their physical body can also change, such as the ear positions, tail position, or raising their hackles. They may also freeze when they are stressed and compress down to be small and still. They may become "busy" by sniffing distractedly or wandering and not paying attention to you. They may also increase vocalizations of whining or barking. All these things and more can be signs that your dog is stressed.

Next time you are in the company of dogs, see how many of these you can identify. Are they in a normal context for this dog or out of context and therefore, probably a stress behavior? It is very important that you can identify and interpret dog body language, as—I repeat—this is the primary way dogs communicate with us.

Once you identify that your dog is stressed, then you need to do something about it. First, identify the stressor, or at least attempt to, as it is not always possible to know the exact stressor for your dog since they can't directly communicate this to us. Then help your dog through the perceived stressful situation. Do this by managing the stressor, removing the stressor, or removing the dog from the stressor. Knowing what the stressor is—for example, fireworks—will help you avoid the stressor or be more prepared to work through it the next time.

Assistance dogs are dogs, who can be stressed by various things such as loud or sudden noises, changes in routine, *your* stress level, busy environments, people or dogs approaching too quickly, being asked too much of them, being uncertain about what to do, etc. It will take time to learn *what stresses your individual dog*. This list is not comprehensive, and your dog may or may not be stressed by the things on this list. However, it is incredibly important for your working relationship and the success of your team that you can identify when your dog is stressed.

Stress also comes in various degrees. Your dog's stress level could be only a little concerning, or your dog could be very stressed, to the point of completely shutting down, unable to work, unable to take treats, and even having to eliminate their bowels. To minimize these effects, it's very important that you can identify the degree of stress your dog is under. Additionally, by listening to your dog, responding when the dog expresses a need for your help, you will be able to set your team up for success and build an incredible bond and partnership.

If the dog is *very* stressed *and you don't know the stressor*, you may need to remove yourself and your dog from the situation. In doing this, you are showing your dog that you care about them when they are stressed or uncomfortable. Caring for their stress levels and mental and emotional needs is incredibly important. By doing this, you will be able to create a mutually beneficial partnership for life.

🐾 What things will you look for to tell you that your dog is stressed?

🐾 What will you do if you identify that your dog is stressed?

🐾 What benefits and challenges can you add to your pros and cons list?

CHAPTER 6

Financial care

Handlers are responsible for financially caring for their assistance dog. The most important aspect of financial care is understanding now, before you commit to this journey, whether you can realistically afford a dog. A dog's everyday care and medical care cost money. These expenses can add up quickly. This section will outline the cost of care for a dog, but it's up to you to do the research and more accurately determine the costs of care in your area. Go to www.understandingassistancedogs. com to download and complete an estimated budget for these costs.

Daily care

Daily care for a dog will include financial consideration for many things. When going through this section, it may be beneficial (or more accurate) to determine what breed or, more importantly, size of dog you would most likely have, as this will impact the costs of their care. The most common types of assistance dogs are Labrador retrievers, poodles, or golden retrievers although any breed of dog or size (pending they can physically perform the skills you need), including mutts, can be an assistance dog.

The cost of equipment can be minimal or expensive depending on the equipment you need. All dogs will need at minimum a leash and collar. Some dogs also need other gear like a Gentle Leader®, Halti®, or body harness' to assist their loose-leash walking ability. If you have a dog who wears a mobility harness as part of their skills, this is another expense. High-quality, ergonomically sound mobility harnesses can cost anywhere from three hundred to seven hundred US dollars (possibly more).

A dog will also need supplies for daily living such as two bowls, one for food and one for water, an appropriate-sized crate, and poop bags. More optional accessories that you don't necessarily need but people often like to have include dog beds, toys, Nylabone® chews, KONG® food dispensers, snuffle mats, and other enrichment items. Although they are optional, people typically have some, so it's good to include consideration for what you can financially afford.

So far, these financial considerations have been items that you may only need to buy once—or twice if a replacement is needed. These are essentially one-time costs for an assistance dog.

Other necessary purchases for a dog's daily care are more regular, such as food. As mentioned previously, it's important to not buy the cheapest food or switch food depending on what's on sale. Cheap dog food typically does not have quality ingredients. If you feed your dog quality food, you will have a healthier, happier dog, able to work for you better and longer.

🐾 Do your research: what are your top three dog food brands?

🐾 For each of these three, what is the cost per bag?

🐾 Can you estimate how many bags you will go through per year? What would be the estimated cost per year?

Next, think about each part of daily care for a dog; start to determine whether you will need assistance with these physically and if you can financially afford to have others help you with them. This includes grooming, waste cleanup, dog walking, and house cleaning services.

Grooming. Are you physically able to groom your dog independently? This includes bathing (quarterly), brushing their coat (weekly) and teeth (daily), cleaning their ears (fortnightly), and clipping their nails (weekly). If so, you will need to buy grooming supplies, including brushes, toothpaste, dog shampoo, ear cleaner, nail clippers or a Dremel, etc. If you are not physically able to groom your dog, do you have someone willing to help you do this? Otherwise, you will need to take the dog to a groomer.

Depending on the type of dog you have, the necessity of brushing their fur or clipping their hair can vary greatly. Grooming services will depend on these factors, so do your research on various breeds' grooming needs. Additionally, the costs of grooming services in different areas can vary greatly, so plan now and prepare for these costs.

🐾 Based on the breed you are likely to get, what grooming are you able to do yourself, and what would you need assistance with?

🐾 Do your research: what do three different groomers charge in your area and what services are included?

Waste cleanup. Dogs will empty their bowels, or poop, daily, sometimes multiple times per day. Think about where your dog will relieve themselves and whether you will physically be able to get there to clean it up in all weather conditions.

The two main places where dogs relieve themselves are in their yard or designated toileting spot and somewhere on a walk. Assistance dogs may also relieve themselves outside of stores or public establishments. You will need to pick up their solid waste right away. However, if you are at home, you may have more liberty to leave it for a little while. In any situation, consider how you can access their waste. If you are unstable on uneven surfaces, like grass or gravel, how will you get to that spot? If you are in a wheelchair, can you reach it?

You also need to consider your ability and dexterity to physically pick up the solid waste. If this will be challenging for you, there are tools on the market, such as various designs of pooper scoopers, to assist with waste cleanup. Another option, if you can financially afford it, is hiring someone to come to your house to clean up your dog's waste regularly.

The location of your dog's toileting area and how you clean it up is typically not a limiting factor to getting an assistance dog, though it may require creativity on your part. Often handlers can regulate the length of leash they provide to keep their dog reasonably close or use various tools to assist in cleanup. Sometimes guide dogs are trained to wear a waste-collecting harness so it's easier for their handler to clean up after them.

🐾 How do you plan to manage waste cleanup for a dog?

🐾 If you need a waste-cleanup service or device, what will this cost?

Dog walking. Exercising and walking your dog should be your responsibility as the handler. However, there are times when you may need assistance with this; for example, when recovering from hip surgery. In situations like this, do you have someone who can assist you to walk your dog, or will you need to hire a dog walker? Dog walkers charge various rates in different locations, so use the space below to write out what the going rate for a dog walker is in your area.

🐾 Do your research: what do three different dog walkers cost per walk in your area?

If you need a dog walker, it is your responsibility to teach the dog walker (or family/friend who is assisting you) how to properly walk your dog and assist that person with distraction management for your dog. The dog's good loose-leash walking should be maintained by whoever is walking the dog.

Housekeeping. Consider whether the addition of a dog into your life may necessitate hiring a housekeeper. Do you already rely on a housekeeper to keep your home clean? If so, will the addition of a dog (especially one that sheds) into your life make you need to increase the number of times the housekeeper comes? Another option to manage shed fur is to get a robot vacuum or other cleaning-assistive device.

🐾 If you think a housekeeper is necessary, do your research and determine what three different housekeepers charge in your area.

🐾 If you will need a robot vacuum or other extra cleaning equipment, what will that cost?

As you can start to see, dogs can be very expensive, and we aren't done yet!

Medical care

You must plan for medical expenses before you ever bring a dog home. At minimum, dogs need yearly veterinary checkups to ensure they are healthy and to keep them current on all necessary vaccinations and preventatives.

First, you will need to determine what veterinary clinic you want to go to. This should be local so it's easy to access and with a veterinarian and staff that you can trust and feel comfortable communicating with. If you don't have a dog currently or haven't had a dog for a while, it is a good idea to get recommendations from friends and family who have dogs to see which local veterinarians they would recommend.

🐾 Do your research: list three local vets you would feel comfortable taking a dog to and their cost for an annual vet visit.

Annual vet visits, when working dogs get professional eyes on them, are important. As you will see your dog every day, it can be harder to notice subtle changes, compared to someone knowledgeable who knows your dog through fairly infrequent visits. Additionally, during these visits, your vet may be able to catch any conditions or issues early to treat them or prevent them before they become a problem that potentially stops your dog from working. This early detection can also help keep the dog working longer. Therefore, make sure you can financially afford, at minimum, a yearly vet visit. Even better, if you can afford it, take the dog every six months for a checkup.

Additionally, if your dog is sick, has fleas or something similar, they should not be working until they're better. Therefore, always ensure your dog has the necessary vaccinations (like rabies) and preventatives (like heartworm prevention and flea and tick prevention) to help keep them working their best. Keeping your dog healthy is important not just for the dog's well-being but also for your ability to use the dog to help mitigate your disability.

🐾 What is the average cost of vaccinations?

🐾 What is the average cost of flea and tick preventatives?

🐾 What is the average cost of heartworm preventatives?

These are all regular, predictable expenses. However, emergencies also occur. Being prepared for them involves having a financial and physical plan. You do not want to be in an emergency situation when you, for the first time, think about what you will do and how you will pay for it. This is an added stress that you do not need in an already stressful time. So plan now!

🐾 Go to www.understandingassistancedogs.com to download and complete an emergency action plan.

First, you need to locate the local emergency veterinary clinic. Which emergency vet is closest to home, work, school, or other places that you frequent? When you arrive, most emergency clinics will charge an upfront fee for seeing your dog, which could be a couple of hundred dollars. Then based on their evaluation and what is needed to care for your dog, the cost can increase dramatically, easily reaching thousands of dollars. Therefore, take time in the space below to determine how you will pay for an emergency. It is best to have designated funds put away now for these situations.

🐾 How will I pay for an emergency medical expense for my dog?

🐾 Where will this money come from?

Next, you need to put an emergency plan in place for any and all situations that might come up. For example, how will you get your dog to the vet if you are alone, without a vehicle, unable to lift your dog into the vehicle, etc.? Are there people in your social support network you can ask for help in these situations who live close to you and can drop what they are doing to come help? Make sure these people are aware that they are your emergency support and backup in these situations. Confirm that they are comfortable in this role and agree to it.

After you return home from an emergency vet trip, your dog should not work until they have fully recovered. During this time, you may need assistance in caring for your dog, depending on what the situation is or the care that was provided or continues to need to be provided. If you are unable to do so, do you have friends or family who can assist you in caring for a sick or injured dog? Additionally, since your dog will be unable to assist you as they recover, will you need extra assistance around the house or in public? Discuss with your support network now what their ability will be to help you in such situations.

Also consider who will assist you to care for your dog if *you* have a medical emergency. For example, if you are in the hospital. Remember, it is not the hospital staff's responsibility to care for your dog, it is yours, with the assistance from your support network. Your assistance dog should not be staying with you in the hospital unless you can *fully* care for them while there. Typically, it's better to leave assistance dogs at home where someone in the support network can care for them.

🐾 Who will care for your dog if you experience an emergency? This should not be the same person who's caring for you.

It is imperative that you know now that you can *financially* care for a dog. Do your research on what things cost in your area to make sure you are prepared and have savings to help with unexpected expenses that arise. If you can't meet any of these financial needs, your dog will not be able to do their job properly. *And* it will be inhumane.

🐾 Discuss with your friends and family what aspects of financial care they believe will be the most challenging for you when caring for a dog.

🐾 What benefits and challenges can you add to your pros and cons list?

CHAPTER 7

Personal lifestyle considerations

If managed correctly and with the right dog, an assistance dog can fit into many lifestyles. However, not all, so your lifestyle is important to consider—everything from your physical ability to reward a dog to how often you go out in public. This chapter will help you determine if an assistance dog will fit into your lifestyle and could be the right tool for you.

Most of the lifestyle factors discussed are on spectrums; therefore, it is incredibly difficult to say definitively if an assistance dog will or will not be beneficial for you. Holistically consider these factors with everything else discussed throughout Part 2. Make sure to keep filling out your pros and cons list as you go through this chapter.

On the spectrum of "outgoing social butterfly" to diagnosed with agoraphobia, where do you fall? If you fall anywhere from an outgoing social butterfly to experiencing mild discomfort in public, an assistance dog may be a great tool for you. However, if you fall between mild discomfort in public to severe social anxiety or agoraphobia, an assistance dog may not be the right tool.

This is because, as discussed in Chapter 3, dogs will draw attention to you. Everywhere you go, people will look at you; they might point at you or your dog, possibly follow you, take unsolicited pictures, and/or want to chat. Assistance dog handlers experience this regularly. The conversations can be very positive or negative, and either way they can be overwhelming, even for people without social anxiety (remember Joe and Max from Chapter 3?). Therefore, if you are very uncomfortable in public already, an assistance dog will make this worse, not better.

Prospective handlers often feel that an assistance dog will help them feel more comfortable or confident in public, and that might be true. For people who feel a mild discomfort in public, it may be an asset. However, if you have more severe social anxiety, an assistance dog can exacerbate it due to the added social interactions that will occur. Honestly consider for yourself whether an assistance dog will exacerbate these feelings, potentially significantly, due to the quantity of social interactions drawn to you.

Additionally, if you have moderate to severe anxiety in general, an assistance dog in itself can increase that anxiety. There can be a lot of internal and external pressure that handlers feel. These anxieties often surround ideas of your dog's progress; for example, that your dog isn't good enough, isn't learning quickly enough, is getting it wrong. Other anxieties occur from ideas about yourself as a handler; for example, that you aren't good enough, or that you don't deserve an assistance dog. This thought could also arise from perceived external pressure; for example, that your dog isn't as good as another assistance dog you know, or the assistance dog organization you are working with doesn't think you are a good trainer, or it thinks you are not learning quickly enough or is not proud of you or happy with your pace of training. These anxieties can arise whether you train your own dog or get a trained dog from an assistance dog organization and can impact your ability to successfully work with an assistance dog.

If you believe you will be prone to more anxiety-provoking thoughts while working with an assistance dog, this path may not be the right tool for you currently. However, that is not to say that an assistance dog couldn't be a good tool for you in the future, once you have devoted time and energy to working on your ability to overcome or minimize social anxieties. A professional, such as a therapist, can be instrumental in leading you through this process and helping you develop strategies to manage your anxiety in triggering situations.

Throughout my experience, I recommended that handlers—before committing to working with an assistance dog—have minimal anxiety in public or currently have tools to successfully work through these anxieties. If a handler doesn't and begins working with an assistance dog anyway, the handler often decides it's too much to deal with and stops taking the dog out in public. This reduces the dog's effectiveness and can quickly undo all of the training. Therefore, the next thing to consider is how frequently you go out in public.

🐾 What strategies will you use to handle the social pressure of having an assistance dog?

🐾 What strategies will you use to handle the internal anxieties of being an assistance dog handler?

On the spectrum of "I never leave my home" to "I only sleep at my home," how often do you spend time in public? This is an important consideration in determining if an assistance dog is the right tool for you because a considerable benefit of having an assistance dog is that it can assist you in public. If you rarely go in public or always have other support in public, an assistance dog who has public access may be unnecessary.

For an assistance dog, going in public and feeling comfortable there is a skill that took years to acquire. If you don't go into public venues often enough together, this aptitude can be lost, and the next time you venture out in public, your dog might be very uncomfortable, display many stress behaviors, or act inappropriately, no longer being at ease in a public environment.

Assistance dogs need regular outings into the community— at least one time per week—but more is better. If they don't get those outings, they can lose their public-access skills. This was exemplified during the Covid-19 pandemic when handlers were not going into the community as much. It can also happen for people who have many bad days and can't care for or utilize their dog during these days, including taking them in public.

Therefore, consider how often you go into the community, especially alone. It's important. If every time you go into the community, you have someone with you to assist, an assistance dog may be unnecessary. If you determine you don't need the dog in public, it could still provide you with great skills around the home. Some assistance dog organizations have started placing dogs for people who don't need an assistance dog in the community but do at home. This type of dog doesn't have a consistent name yet, but it has been called a "skilled home companion," "skilled home helpmate," or various other names. Dogs who don't enjoy public outings often get paired with people who don't need an assistance dog to accompany them in public. These dogs, however, are just as good at performing skills in the home. It is important to note that these dogs are *not* emotional support animals because they have trained tasks they perform to mitigate a person's disability, where emotional support animals don't have any trained tasks.

🐾 Do you go in public often enough to need an assistance dog with public access?

🐾 Do you need support when you go in public? Will your dog have a job to do in public?

It is important to consider, on the spectrum of *all your days are good* to *all your days are bad*, where does your average day/week/month fall on this spectrum? The number and severity of your bad days are especially important to consider. Remember, an assistance dog is not a magical unicorn that will fix all your problems and eliminate bad days. You will still have bad days physically, mentally, or emotionally. An assistance dog will not change this.

If your bad days are so bad you can't get out of bed or are so numerous that most of your week or month is a "bad day," then an assistance dog may not be the right tool for you. After all, realistically consider your ability to care for a dog on your worst days. It is okay for a family member or friend to care for your dog *some* of the time; however, you want to limit this as much as possible.

You also need to consider the added effort it will take to care for the dog on your bad days and how many spoons it will require. There will be some days when you need more from your assistance dog than they can supply—and, contrarily, especially if you experience extreme differences between good and bad days, on some days you'll provide more for your dog's needs than you get back in return. Overall, this dynamic should be balanced. If the spoons the dog is regularly requiring from you add up to more than the time and work that having the assistance dog saves you, then this option is probably not the right choice.

This has been demonstrated over and over with handlers. For example, Norah had been training her own assistance dog, Kirby, for a few years. Due to her disability being very variable—with some days where she could barely get out of bed and other days where she felt fine—her relationship with Kirby was unbalanced and strained. Although they had been working together for years, Kirby was not yet reliable in the skills he had been taught. This unreliability derived from Norah's inability to train, reinforce, or be consistent during training because it was regularly requiring more "spoons" from Norah than she had to spare. This not only slowed the training progression but was possibly making Norah's already unstable condition worse because Kirby needed more from Norah than he was giving back most of the time. This was not a mutually beneficial relationship; it proved ultimately unsuccessful.

To avoid having this happen to you, it's important that most of your days aren't bad days and that even on your bad days you can sufficiently care for and utilize an assistance dog. If you have a lot of bad days before getting an assistance dog, consider what you could change in your life to help decrease the number of bad days there are. Are you utilizing all the resources, therapies, and support currently available to you?

🐾 How many bad days do you have per month?

🐾 Are you *realistically* able to sufficiently care for a dog on your bad days?

Next, it's important to consider your ability to physically handle and work with an assistance dog. By this I mean your ability to do things like hold or clip a leash, reward with treats, and communicate with a dog.

All these things can be challenges, depending on your disability. However, dogs are adaptable, and with a little innovation, so are you. If, for example, you can't physically hold a leash because of grip strength, handlers have attached the leash to their powerchair. If physically manipulating the clip on the leash or collar is challenging for you due to dexterity, there are alternatives on the market that you can test to see if they will work for you. Additionally, if limited hand dexterity prevents you from giving treats by hand, there are other ways to reward a dog such as using a lick stick or squeeze tube filled with yummy treats. There are also automated treat dispensers on the market that may be suitable for your needs.

🐾 What challenges do you envision having physically when working with an assistance dog? Think realistically and write them down. Ask your support system for their observations as well.

🐾 Do your research and see if there are ways you can make adaptations for yourself or your dog. How can you overcome these challenges? Be creative!

This is a great topic to discuss with your support network, who may have innovative ideas on ways to overcome these challenges. Alternatively, talk with a professional in the industry to see how other handlers have overcome similar challenges. Some resources such as those described above can be found on www.understandingassistancedogs.com under the resources tab.

If your verbal communication ability is limited, either in clarity, volume, or ability to speak at all, this can typically be overcome, as dogs are adaptable. They just need to be taught the best way to communicate with you. Dogs have learned to understand sign language and talker boards, believe it or not, and nonstandard human speech. Therefore, don't let your limited verbal communication ability stop you from getting an assistance dog. Rather, get creative and think through ways that you can teach a dog to understand you.

✿ What kind of communication will you use with an assistance dog?

Next, as mentioned, assistance dogs will require maintenance training for life. Therefore, it is important to consider your ability to maintain their training. Again, assistance dogs are not robots, where once programmed to do something, they can do it for life. They need practice to maintain their skills and exhibit proper behavior in public.

If this practice is not provided, you will experience challenges similar to what Patricia experienced, even if your disability isn't as severe. Matched with Zeus, an assistance dog trained by a qualified organization, Patricia, however, struggled with memory challenges and learning disabilities that limited her ability to remember to reinforce the dog for good behavior. Therefore, over time, Zeus had started to lose his ability to perform tasks or only performed them when he felt like it. Patricia's intellectual disability was severe enough that she needed assistance with or reminders of most things regarding Zeus' care as well. This led Patricia's support network to step in and assist in caring for the dog. However, as Zeus' trained abilities were declining, he was at the same time preferring to spend all his time with the support network that was caring for him. This led to severe challenges in the dog/handler relationship and the dog's ability to work.

Irrespective of where or how you get an assistance dog, it will be incredibly important that you be consistent in maintaining rules when it comes to their care and training. If you are unable to adhere to rules, your assistance dog will quickly lose the training it worked so diligently and devotedly to acquire.

These rules include making sure the dog is not pulling, but instead is walking with a nice, loose leash and responding to cues the first time. The dog should, by all means, not barge through doorways or eat food off the ground, especially in public. One of the most important rules to maintain as a handler, or it will cause you and other handlers a lot of grief, is not to allow people to pet your dog in public. All these rules aim to increase your safety and should be practiced for life. Without rules, dogs will take advantage of you or will instead do what they want (pulling on a leash, rushing the door, greeting everyone, etc.), which is not conducive to being an assistance dog.

If maintaining rules or training is difficult for you because of, for example, memory challenges, what strategies do you currently have in place to mitigate memory issues? Could these techniques be applied to working with an assistance dog? If you don't have such techniques in place, develop them before getting an assistance dog, as you don't want to forget to care for your dog or not follow training guidelines, etc. Otherwise, your dog will take advantage of you and quickly regress in training.

🐾 Are you able to maintain your dog's training—committed to maintaining it and being consistent?

🐾 What benefits and challenges can you add to your pros and cons list?

CHAPTER 8

Considerations for other members of your life

Considerations for family members in the home

Social support is a key factor in the success of an assistance dog team. I hope your support network is as excited as you to start this journey. Handlers with good social support typically find the journey smoother than handlers with less social support or with unsupportive people in their social circle because you will probably need your support network's help at some point.

As you have a disability significant enough to benefit from having an assistance dog, perhaps there are aspects of the dog's care that you cannot physically do yourself. This may occur semi-regularly, primarily only on your bad days, or just when you have gone out of town and decided not to bring your dog (which is perfectly fine).

During these times, you will need support from family or friends to meet all your dog's needs. This is okay. It is important and necessary to have a support network of people who can assist you. If you don't have any social support you can rely on, I guarantee that you will have more challenges with an assistance dog than those who have a strong social support network. It is so important that I believe if you don't have *any* social support, then an assistance dog is not the right option for you.

An active and supportive social network often helps facilitate a smooth transition for you and the assistance dog initially and assists in the lifetime success of the team. Seemingly contradictory, it is more important than you probably realize for your support network to be hands off with the assistance dog. During the first days, weeks, and even months that an assistance dog is in your home, your family needs to limit their interaction with the dog—in this way, they are helping you form a bond and showing the dog that you are the person to go to for all their needs to be met and fun to be had. This is especially important initially because a dog will prefer to interact with the person who is feeding them, playing with them, showing them affection, etc. If you only ask your dog to work and don't provide any of the other positive things, it will be hard for the dog to want to bond with you and eventually possibly work for you.

Therefore, you want to save these positive experiences for yourself. Other family and friends' interactions with your dog should be kept minimal, as you need this time for the dog to *think that all good things, insofar as the dog is concerned, come from you.* Even casual affection or attention from other family members can slow your bonding process. This is especially important if your disability does not physically allow you to interact with a dog in the standard way or your support network lives in your home.

If your support network lives in your home, that's great because of the convenience. However, these individuals must not overstep and assist you with everything (or even most things) regarding your dog. If they do, they could accidentally make themselves your dog's favorite person (remember Zeus' relationship with Patricia's support network?). This can likely occur if they feed or play with the assistance dog regularly, which will be detrimental to your bond with the dog.

For example, people with limited arm or hand movement may have minimal ability to physically pet a dog, compared to a person with a normal range of motion. As most dogs really enjoy that type of physical contact, if your partner can (and does) give the dog affection that way, your dog may start to prefer your partner over you. Dogs are adaptable *and will like any physical contact you can give them*, even if it is not standard ear scratches.

Another example involves vision impairments. Assistance dogs are often trained to make eye contact with a human. It's a natural communication signal used in play and lets you know whether you have the dog's attention. Therefore, when a dog is accustomed to making direct eye contact and a vision-impaired handler's ability to make direct eye contact is limited, the lack of reciprocated eye contact can be confusing for dogs initially. For example, a dog will use eye contact to indicate a ball is "over there"—looking at the ball and back at the person. This is important communication in human-dog play. If the handler's partner can give this eye contact, especially during play, the partner may become the preferred play friend and consequently looked to in other situations as well.

A final example: suppose a handler is unable to physically feed their dog. Meals are incredibly important to most dogs; therefore, they will grant high value to whoever provides them. If you physically cannot place the dog's bowl on the ground or in a stand, there are still ways you can create this connection. Typically, assistance dogs are trained to sit and wait to begin eating a meal until they are released to eat it. Therefore, as the handler, you can take this role back by communicating to your dog when it is time to eat by giving the release command, even if you do not physically place the food in front of them.

You may notice that these three examples demonstrated the three most common motivators for dogs: physical affection, play, and food. These are the three ways you will begin to form a bond; therefore, they are the actions and responsibilities you want to keep for yourself as much as possible initially.

Each of these examples also demonstrates how simple it can be for your dog to learn to prefer another person over you, especially if you are not able to meet all these needs independently. If these situations describe you, it will be especially important that your family does not interfere more than necessary with your dog, especially initially. For this reason, it is particularly important to know now if your family will respect your need for them to be hands off initially. If they can't, they will slow or potentially derail the bonding process.

Therefore, as much as you can, you need to care for your dog independently. If you believe this will be challenging, I recommend brainstorming with your support network to find as many creative and adaptive ways as possible for you to do things for your dog instead of relying on help. This will allow you to be more independent in working with the dog and form a stronger bond.

🐾 What are some challenges in which you will need help from other people when caring for your dog?

🐾 How can you get creative and possibly do these things for yourself? Chat with your social support network about these challenges and how you can be creative to overcome them.

🐾 Will your family understand and respect your need for them to keep their hands off and distance themselves from your dog initially? How can you help them understand?

Additionally, if you have kids, consider whether they are at an age and understanding where they won't interfere with the dog's work. Think about how you may need to manage your kids around the dog and your ability to do so. How can you make sure your dog is comfortable around your kids and that they are not being overwhelming or interfering with the dog's alone time? How will your kids react when the dog is assisting you? Will they show respect for the dog's work and not be a distraction?

Overall, you need to have a support network to assist you when needed. These same people also need to understand that they need to be hands off, especially initially, to help you through the bonding and learning process with your dog. If you do not believe your support network will respect this, an assistance dog may not be the right tool for you. Make sure you talk openly with your support network about their role in your assistance dog journey.

Considerations for other animals in the home

Your current animals are part of the family. As their owner, you have the responsibility to ensure they feel safe and secure in their own home. They, therefore, deserve consideration for *how an assistance dog could fit into their life, as well as yours*. Not all animals will welcome living with a new dog. Therefore, before you decide to work with an assistance dog, you need to determine:

1. Are your other animals comfortable living with a dog?
2. Will the other animals cause interference with the assistance dog's job?

3. How will you transfer the care of other animals to another family member? Who will this be?

Make sure, in advance, that all your current animals are comfortable around dogs. More specifically, make sure they are comfortable with a dog who is like what your assistance dog will be like.

To do this I recommend reaching out to see if anyone you know has a dog of similar energy and size, as you expect your assistance dog to be. Typically, this is a medium to large dog that is relatively young (one to three years old) and energetic. If a friend has a dog of the same breed but is outside the energy or age range, it won't be a good comparison. For example, an eight-week-old puppy or an eight-year-old dog will not provide you with a good understanding of how your pets will react to an assistance dog.

If you don't test this out, you could end up in a situation like Nancy. Nancy received an assistance dog named Pluto from an assistance dog organization. When Pluto moved home with her, it was into a home that had a cat with minimal experience with dogs; she was used to being the only animal. The cat, Bootsie, was not pleased to have Pluto in her space, spending a lot of time with her human. This caused conflict in the cat, who would lash out at the dog, swatting when the dog crossed her path. Bootsie was very bold around Pluto and started to interfere with the dog's job to alert Nancy to sounds in her environment. If Pluto attempted to show Nancy where the sound was coming from and it was near Bootsie, the dog became hesitant and conflicted because it didn't want to be smacked by the cat. As Pluto was a hearing alert dog, the alerts were unpredictable;

therefore, Pluto and Bootsie had to be separated behind baby gates, closed doors or monitored very closely continuously. This caused added stress for everyone involved, as they didn't want to rehome their cat, although it was a possibility they considered.

Take time now to determine if your cat is bold like Bootsie or will hide for days when a dog is around. To do this, identify a dog in your support network of a similar size and energy level to your potential assistance dog, and invite that dog over to your house to see how your animals react. If possible, to get a true understanding of the magnitude of stress having a new dog move in could cause your other animals, dog-sit for a few days. That way, you can realistically simulate the effect on your current animals. By having the dog come to your home, you are, as well, minimizing the additional stressors your animals would experience if taken to a new location to meet a dog.

This test will give you valuable information on how your animals might react when an assistance dog first moves home. Therefore, take notes (video if possible) on how your animals behave initially, and over time with the dog present. Examples of things to take note of include:

- How long did your cat hide under the bed? The next twelve hours?
- Did your dog hide behind the couch?
- Did the hamsters run on their wheel endlessly until the dog was gone?
- Did your cat come out puffed up ready to fight?
- Did your dog start running around the house with zoomies?

- Did your bird continuously talk/sing the entire time the dog was present?
- Did your cat swipe or hiss at the dog?
- Did your dog become submissive or start marking?
- Did your animal return to "normal" behavior while the dog was there? If so, how long did this take?
- If your animal did not return to "normal" while the dog was there, how long did it take for your animal to return to "normal" behaviors after the dog left?

Many of the items listed above are stress behaviors. These are important to take into consideration because it shows you how much stress your animals could be under if you add an assistance dog to your home environment.

Objectively determine if your pets will be accepting of a new dog in the home. If the stress and unease seem insurmountable for your pets, remember, it is *animal abuse* to force them to live the rest of their life in a constant state of stress because you want an assistance dog. Therefore, seriously consider whether you are willing to rehome them or wait until after they pass to get an assistance dog. These are situations you need to consider now, rather than when the dog has already moved home with you.

Let's say your animals will be okay with adding a dog into the home. Next, consider whether your animals will cause any interference with your assistance dog's job. Interference may occur if other animals are bullying the assistance dog and making it feel unsafe working independently in your home. Thinking back to Nancy's story, because Pluto got swatted at by Bootsie each time he crossed the cat's path, Pluto never want to cross the cat's path. However, to alert the handler, crossing Bootsie's path was sometimes necessary. Such situations could also prevent the dog from pressing the emergency help button or getting juice from the fridge. If the dog is scared to do this, then success will be impossible; or the dog might not want to work for you while the other animal is around.

This is a huge problem for you, and you have a few choices. First, to continuously manage the locations of your pets and the assistance dog so they are not interacting, maybe you block off portions of your house, keeping the pets and the assistance dog separated. This can cause a lot of added stress to you, as well as on the pets being confined, when they previously weren't. The other option is, as just mentioned above, to rehome the other animal or wait until it passes before getting an assistance dog. Again, this is better to think about now instead of when the assistance dog arrives.

If you will be working with a trainer or an assistance dog organization, truthfully share your experience of introducing your current pets to a dog (and any video of the interactions) so they can help you determine the best course of action.

Now that you know your other animals will be comfortable with a dog in their space and won't interfere with the assistance dog's work, you need to start transitioning the care of the pets to another person. If you are not the one to currently care for the pets, great!

If you currently care for the pets, it's important to transition this responsibility to another family member when possible. This will help your animals not feel as stressed about all the changes that happen when you bring an assistance dog home.

If you don't do this ahead of time, they may feel "abandoned" by you as you take on the full responsibility of caring for the assistance dog and focus on building a relationship with them.

Therefore, be proactive and shift the responsibilities for feeding, exercising, and grooming the animals to another person. This is for the same reason that you want to keep all the good things coming from you with your assistance dog. We want all the good things for your animals to come from another person now. This transition should happen well before your assistance dog arrives home so that your animals can form a stronger bond with the other person, thus easing the transition for everyone.

🐾 How do you think your other animals will react to having a dog in the home?

🐾 Who will care for your other animals?

🐾 What benefits and challenges can you add to your pros and cons list?

CHAPTER 9

Home life considerations

As you consider whether an assistance dog is the right tool for you, ensure that your home is conducive to having a dog and determine whether you can care for a dog in your current home. This starts with ensuring your home environment is stable and safe.

Dogs thrive in stability and predictability, where they feel secure, and able to perform better work for you. They tend to not enjoy the stress and change of moving to a new home. If you are planning to move shortly or if you have just moved, it is best to wait to get an assistance dog until after you have fully settled in. After moving, typically, there is a lot of chaos of unpacking, rearranging, and finding your routine and new normal which dogs don't enjoy.

Additionally, other aspects of your life should be relatively stable. No upcoming or recent job changes, major life transitions, etc. If you wait until your life is stable, you will have more success working with an assistance dog. Mark is a great example of this. Mark waited ten years after initially considering whether to get an assistance dog. Initially he explored the option just after graduating from college. At that time, he'd just begun an internship, with unknown prospects for working there full time in the future, and had just purchased a house that was being remodeled to make it more accessible for his needs. He had a lot going on, a lot of changes and instability in his life. Thankfully, he decided to wait to get an assistance dog until things were stable in his home and career. Looking back, everyone involved believes this was the right choice and is grateful that he waited, as it decreased the stress he would have experienced and has resulted in a successful team.

Just as Mark did, it is important to consider all aspects of your home life before adding an assistance dog to it. Assistance dogs should not be "outside dogs." They should comfortably fit into your home. After all, they cannot help you if they do not have access to you. I am not saying that they need to always be in the same room as you, but they should be able to get to you where you are, preferably not through a shut door they cannot open. Therefore, consider where in your home environment you will have your dog eat, sleep, and toilet. Do you have sufficient space for each of these? Are they accessible to you?

Dogs can eat and drink wherever you put their bowls, but typically they should be in a place that gives you easy access to clean and fill them. Often, this is in the kitchen or dining room area but can be in other places, like a laundry or mud room, depending on the layout of your home. If you have other pets with food bowls, consider where in relation to each other they are. It is best if the food bowls are separated so there is no feeling of competition around mealtimes and food.

🐾 Where will you put your dog's food and water bowls?

Dogs can typically fall asleep anywhere. They like to sleep on dog beds, on furniture, or in their crate. Dog beds are not necessary but a luxury that handlers often buy (sometimes multiple) for their dog.

It will be up to you if the dog is allowed on the furniture or the bed. Both are perfectly acceptable if that's what you want. However, if you want an off-bed, off-furniture policy, it's important to set this rule before the dog gets to your home. This way avoids confusion if later you decide to make the bed off limits.

Also, it's a great idea to have a crate for your dog, a designated spot where they know they can rest without being asked to do skills for you. If you get an assistance dog from an assistance dog organization, the dog will most likely already be crate trained, and it will be your job to keep up this skill, as it's an important one to help prevent separation anxiety and is convenient for people who may need to watch your dog for you from time to time.

🐾 Write out what house rules you want to enforce. For example, will you allow a dog on the furniture?

Your dog will need a toileting spot outside. Of these three considerations, this is the most important one to think about now. It can be helpful if their toileting area is consistent. Dogs taken to the same area to toilet every time learn what's expected of them in that physical area. This is especially important for assistance dogs because you need to know if they are "empty" before taking them in public.

Importantly, your dog's toileting area should be easily accessible to you, as you will need to go there in early morning, late at night, and multiple times throughout the day. Consider whether it is safe for you to get to this area in all weather conditions. If, for example, you have to walk up and down a full flight of stairs each time you take your dog outside to relieve itself but stairs are difficult or potentially unsafe for you to navigate, this will be very challenging and potentially unsafe, especially if the dog has an urgent need to go and is therefore disregarding their good leash manners.

In a fenced-in yard, toileting is typically much easier than walking your dog outside each time to toilet. If you do not have a fenced-in yard but have easy access to the yard, consider whether you can use a tie-out or a long line to secure your dog, so they have more freedom when they toilet but is still confined to a designated space.

🐾 Where will you toilet your dog? Be specific.

🐾 How realistic is it for you to get to the toileting spot multiple times per day?

Considerations for landlords and homeowners' associations

In the case of a landlord or a homeowners' association (HOA), expect more challenges than if you own your home and there is no HOA. I hope you don't have challenges with either; however, as assistance dogs are not well understood by the general public, many landlords and HOAs that have had no experience with members or tenants having an assistance dog may be unsure of what their rights are, what your rights are, and the applicable laws.

As the laws are different internationally, make sure you check your local laws in these contexts. Within the United States, assistance dogs are protected under the Fair Housing Act. This means, as mentioned earlier but it bears repeating, that an assistance dog handler cannot be denied housing because of having an assistance dog, even if the property has a rule that no dogs are allowed or have breed or size restrictions.

If you decide that an assistance dog is the right tool for you, consider giving your landlord or HOA advance notice. How far in advance is up to you, but it may be beneficial to wait until you have a more solid idea of the date your dog will be moving in. If you are renting from a large company that has experience with assistance dogs, they might have a few pieces of paperwork to be filled out.

Although the company can't prevent you from getting an assistance dog, this advance notice is a courtesy, allowing them to do any research they feel is necessary. They will appreciate this, as they may have a lot of questions for you to better understand what their rights are, what your rights are, and how they can support the best outcome for everyone involved, including other tenants.

A common concern they will have is the perception from other homeowners or tenants when they see a dog on the property. One way they can prevent any misconception is by sending notifications to other homeowners or tenants, making them aware that they may see you with an assistance dog on the property. This way, they can prevent complaints from other tenants who see you with a dog but may not have realized it is an assistance dog (because it doesn't need to be identifiable as an assistance dog to relieve itself outside). By sending out this general notice, the landlord or HOA is trying to prevent other members from thinking your dog is a companion dog and wanting to get one too.

Another concern or request they may have involves where you can and cannot take your dog to relieve itself. It is best to figure this out before the dog comes home as it can save you a lot of stress once the dog has moved in. If their request for your dog's toileting location is unreasonable, ask for accommodation, as the toileting location needs to be easily accessible to you, even on your bad days.

In general, when dealing with landlords or HOAs, be open and honest. By giving them advance notice, you can help ease any possible tension in the long run.

Considerations for hazards in the home

Before your dog moves in, make sure your home is dog safe. Even if you currently have a pet dog, double-check. A dog entering a new home will be curious and may try to ingest normally uninteresting objects. Therefore, remove or minimize any hazards, including dangerous areas, objects, plants, food, chemicals, and medications. You can find a downloadable check list under "supporting materials" at www. understandingassistancedogs.com.

Make sure all areas of your home are safe for your dog. If they are not, make the unsafe areas inaccessible by closing doors or using baby gates. Access to these areas should be allowed under direct supervision only. Places in the home that commonly need supervision are storage areas, areas where other animals' food or litterboxes are kept, along with where the trash is stored.

Doors leading to the outside should always be secure as well. If you need your dog to tug doors open for you, consider whether it is safe for the dog to do this for doors leading to the outside. Once the dog learns this skill and if the door is not locked, the result might be that they go outside at random, whenever they feel like it, which is a major safety hazard. Even if the door only goes into the fenced-in backyard, this is a challenge for you, as now you are competing for your dog's attention against all the fun it could be having outdoors. Therefore, if you need a dog to tug open a door leading to the outside, make sure the door remains locked unless you are presently using the door.

When considering dangerous areas outside the home, it is important to check fencing to make sure the gates are secure, with no broken areas or gaps in the fence. Any tall balconies should have a railing. If you have a pool or hot tub, make sure this area is inaccessible. When unsupervised, these areas are, naturally, dangerous to dogs, especially if they fall in and can't get out independently. Any other areas of standing water or where mold is growing, such as compost areas, should also be blocked off so they don't get sick. Additionally, keep your dog, if unsupervised, away from fireplaces, fire pits, or grills.

Within and outside the home, make sure to remove any plants that are poisonous to dogs. If you absolutely cannot remove them, move them up high, out of reach, or put fencing around them.

Store any harmful objects that you have lying around, or in the dog's potential reach, in a place that is inaccessible to the dog. This includes sharp objects like razors and knives or other dangerous items that when swallowed can cause serious internal damage or death, such as batteries, or even—though you may not have thought about it—rubber bands, floss, etc. You will also want to pick up all the little miscellaneous items that may find themselves on the floor, such as paper clips, twist ties, coins, hair pins, etc. These are easy for a dog to swallow and cause internal damage. Personal items of clothing such as socks or nylons are also tempting for dogs and can be easily swallowed.

Make sure these objects are inaccessible; put them up high in a cupboard, behind a baby gate, or in a locked cabinet.

Other objects that can be dangerous are inappropriate-sized toys. This is something to seriously consider if you have young children or other animals, especially smaller animals, who have toys around the home. If this describes you, make sure all the toys are appropriate for the largest animal in the house. For example, cat toys are small, and a larger dog could easily swallow them, causing an internal blockage. The same with children's toys, as they can be small and tempting for a dog to eat. So keep them out of reach.

Other pet items, especially food, should be kept out of reach of an assistance dog. In general, human food should also be inaccessible to them. However, food may fall, and your dog may get it, so please be aware of foods harmful for dogs, which include fatty food, moldy or spoiled food, bones of small animals like chicken or turkey, breads and yeast, alcohol, chocolate, macadamia nuts, etc.

There may be some human foods that you regularly give your dog, like peanut butter. Make sure these do not have harmful ingredients, such as the sugar substitute xylitol, also known as birch sugar, as an ingredient. This is toxic to dogs and is a common ingredient in peanut butter, gum, and some ice creams.

Just like locking the cupboards that store chemicals from a child, you will want to do this for your dog as well. Do not allow them access to any chemicals, including cleaning products, pesticides or herbicides, insect and rodent control chemicals, gas or oil, tobacco products, etc. If your dog ingests these, it could be potentially life-threatening.

Medications, when given inappropriately or accidentally, can also be incredibly toxic to dogs. Therefore, make sure you know the effect that *each* medication in your home can have on a dog. This includes Tylenol, Aleve, and human-grade vitamins. To prevent any accidents, always keep your medications stored securely in a location that your dog can't access. It is also a good idea to take them over the sink or in other areas where if you drop a pill, it is still inaccessible to your dog.

You must take these dangers seriously, as dogs will be curious when they are in a new home and may find more things to get into than normal.

In the next week, thoroughly go through each area of your home, identifying areas, objects, plants, food, chemicals, and medications that need to be cleaned up, put away, made inaccessible, or otherwise altered to make sure your house is safe for an assistance dog. You can find a list of these under "supporting material" at www.understandingassistancedogs.com.

🐾 After reading this chapter, knowing your home, what are the three most important things should you do to prepare your home for an assistance dog?

🐾 What benefits and challenges can you add to your pros and cons list?

CHAPTER 10

Work and school considerations

Another place that assistance dog handlers commonly bring an assistance dog is to work or school. Therefore, take these locations into consideration when deciding whether an assistance dog is the right tool for you. A multitude of factors, which can be incredibly challenging to navigate, need to be considered. Think very critically about your specific situation.

In this chapter, I provide a starting point of what to consider when determining if an assistance dog *should* go to work or school with you. Remember, just because legally they often *can* doesn't always mean that your dog *should* in terms of the best interest of the dog. Without knowing your context specifically, there is no way I can cover all aspects of what might be involved. Therefore, if you desire to bring an assistance dog to these settings, I recommend you chat with your employer or school and professionals in the industry about your specific situation with an open mind.

The first thing to consider is whether your work/school location is dog safe. Will it expose the dog to hazardous chemicals? Constant loud noises? Is there a high potential for injury? Harm of any sort? If so, the location is not safe, and you should not bring the assistance dog. If there are risks to health, safety, or ability to work, leave your dog at home.

Examples of unsafe locations could include places where chemicals are prominent, such as a laboratory (perhaps, for example, a school chemistry lab/classroom) or chemical plant, or place where heavy machinery or power tools are frequent, such as a construction site or a manufacturing plant. Another unsafe place is an industrial kitchen; say, you work there as a line cook. It would not be an appropriate place to bring an assistance dog (knives or boiling water could be dropped on the dog accidentally, and bringing the dog is not sanitary for the customers). If you work at locations that could be considered unsafe for a dog, it is in everyone's best interest to leave the assistance dog at home. You don't want your dog to be injured on the job because then they can't work for you in the short term, while recovering, or potentially long term.

Next, if the location is safe, you need to consider whether you will be physically able to handle or manage the assistance dog while there. Consider children who work in a triad team, with their parent as a handler; they may not have the physical or mental capability to handle the dog independently at school. Hence, the reason for the adult handler in the first place. Therefore, consider if it is safe for the assistance dog to be handled independently by the child in school.

If not, can someone else assist? Are teachers or one-on-one support for the child willing to support the team in necessary ways while the dog is at school? This will entail conversation with the school and individual employees, so it's best to start these conversations early; that way, you can together try to figure out what is best for all involved.

If you are at work or school and can't physically or safely manage your assistance dog because of your mental capacity or the work you are doing, then it's best to not bring your dog.

If it's safe for your dog to attend work with you and you can manage your dog while there or have support in this regard, then you need to consider how much work the dog will have to get to and leave from this location. When at this location, how much work will the dog have to do? If the answer is "not much"—say, because you have a one-on-one para at school or you have other accommodations at work—then consider: Why do I want to bring an assistance dog with me? You may not need to, and that's okay. Let the dog rest at home, depending on the length of time you will be away.

If you believe it's safe to bring an assistance dog—that you can physically handle the requirements and the dog will have a job to do there—next, you need to consider which locations your dog will be in with you. Do you have an office with a door you can shut or a cubicle they can be in with you? Can the dog have a space next to your desk, or are you constantly moving around on the sales floor? A dog will be happier in a designated spot rather than constantly following you around for your entire shift. If you are constantly moving, realistically consider whether the dog will be more in the way than helpful.

Throughout this thought process, carefully consider the benefit vs burden that having an assistance dog with you will create for you both. If there is more burden (on either party), consider leaving the dog at home. Please don't be selfish in wanting your dog to be with you at work or school if it is not appropriate. Seriously consider what is best or most appropriate for the dog. After all, your goal is to create a mutually beneficial relationship.

Take a moment to write out your best-guess responses to these questions.

🐾 Is your work location safe to bring an assistance dog? Why or why not?

🐾 Are you physically able to handle the assistance dog independently while at work or school? Why or why not?

🐾 If you are unable to physically handle the assistance dog, is someone able to assist you? Why or why not?

🐾 How much work (how many tasks or skills) will your dog need to perform at work or school? What about on the way to or from work or school?

🐾 Where will they be while at work or school with you?

🐾 Based on your responses to the above questions, do you feel it is appropriate for you to bring an assistance dog to work or school?

If you will not need the dog at work or school, for how many hours will you be gone? It is okay to leave your dog home from work or school, crated, for no more than eight hours per day. If you must leave your dog crated for eight hours per day or more, especially multiple days per week, consider whether an assistance dog is the right tool for you.

If, based on your above responses, you do believe an assistance dog would be a benefit to you at work or school and taking them there will be safe for the dog, notify the relevant parties well before the first day you intend to bring them. Just like landlords and HOAs, your employer or school will appreciate advance notice. Similarly, they may have questions or concerns, and if you start this process early, you can work together to figure out the best course for all parties involved.

In a workplace setting, a good person to talk to is human resources, which probably has the most knowledge on accessibility, accommodation, and potentially assistance dogs. Depending on the size of the company, they may have experience with assistance dogs or not. As assistance dogs are not commonplace at most companies, they will appreciate your advance notice so they can look up any laws or requirements that they need to uphold on their end and determine how best to accommodate you.

If you plan to bring your assistance dog to school, there are various people you should notify, depending on the type of school you are going to.

If you are going to an elementary, middle, or high (primary or secondary) school, you will want to notify the school principal or administrators. If you don't also notify your specific teachers, they will do this and most likely share this information with all the teachers in the school. Additionally, an assistance dog often needs to be written into your Individualized Education Plan (IEP) or other plans that document the special accommodations you receive in school. This will take time so plan ahead.

If you are doing postsecondary education, such as in a trade school, university, or college, notify the disability office. You can also notify your academic advisor or other administrators that you feel may be helpful. Depending on the school, they may notify your teachers or professors, while others will rely on you to do it.

If you are attending a college or university and plan to live on campus, the housing department should also be made aware that you plan to bring an assistance dog to the dorms and to your classes. Like landlords and HOAs, they may decide to notify everyone in the dorm. Again, this is to prevent people from seeing a dog and wondering why they can't have a pet on campus. Although this desire of others to want a dog is a concern for the housing department, this is not a reason to deny access to an assistance dog.

Other common concerns that schools and workplaces have involve how to deal with people with dog allergies. This is not as big of a concern as they expect. Dog allergies are brought about through prolonged contact with fur or saliva. Since no one will be petting the assistance dog and the dog should not be close enough to others to lick them, there should be no transmission of fur or saliva to cause an allergic reaction.

You can also assure them that your dog will be well-groomed and clean. Meaning that the dog will not be shedding profusely in their buildings and that the little amount of fur that may be left behind should not be enough to cause anyone an allergic reaction.

Another concern will involve people who fear dogs. One way to deal with this is to reassure them that you will be slowly introducing your assistance dog to the shared environment with them. This is important for your dog, but also for the business/school so no one is overwhelmed. Let them see how great your dog does in their environment slowly, so no one is stressed by the initial experience.

If a person fears dogs, it is acceptable for the employer or school to transfer that person to another classroom or workspace, further away from the dog. As an assistance dog is a piece of medical equipment, the handler has the right to take the dog into the classroom or office space, irrespective of other people's allergies and fears.

There may also be concern about an assistance dog barking or disrupting other customers, employees, or students. Typically, this imagined fear eases once they meet the assistance dog and are impressed with the level of training. If your dog is being disruptive, such as elimination inside or uncontrollable barking, and you are unable to regain control, they have the right to ask you to remove the dog. In that case, you will have to do so. This also applies to public places.

Overall, if you determine that it is appropriate and safe to bring an assistance dog to your workplace or school, it is best to give as much advance notice as possible, allowing the other party time to prepare—thus, helping reduce tension on the first day your dog attends. This also allows all parties to feel more comfortable and confident about having an assistance dog in attendance.

🐾 What benefits and challenges can you add to your pros and cons list?

Takeaways

Many considerations need to be seriously evaluated before working with an assistance dog. All the considerations culminate in answering one question: *Will I be able to form a mutually beneficial relationship with an assistance dog?* This partnership is not all about you. You also need to be confident that you can sufficiently care for an assistance dog in such a way that the relationship benefits you both.

An assistance dog can't assist you or care for you if their needs are not met first—in terms of physical, mental, and emotional health, as well as financial support. In any situations where you may not be able to care for the dog independently, make sure you have a sufficient support system and plan in place. If you do not, you will experience more challenges with an assistance dog, compared to handlers who are prepared.

Beyond this preparation, there are a good deal of other considerations to help you identify whether you can realistically and properly care for an assistance dog before you bring one into your home. For one, make sure your lifestyle, living situation, support system, current animals, and work or school considerations have been addressed and are appropriate. Overall, you need to be certain that you can form a mutually beneficial relationship with an assistance dog.

Part 2 learning objectives

After reading this section you should be able to...

- determine if you can care for an assistance dog physically, mentally, and emotionally.
- determine if you can financially afford an assistance dog.
- determine if your lifestyle is appropriate for utilizing an assistance dog.
- determine if other members of your home will be okay with the addition of an assistance dog.
- prepare your home so it is suitable for an assistance dog.
- prepare to talk with your employer or school about having an assistance dog.

🐾 Do you *honestly* believe you can form a mutually beneficial relationship with an assistance dog?

🐾 Have you been completing your pros and cons list throughout this book? What does your list look like so far? If you haven't started, take time now to write a detailed list of all your pros and cons regarding working with an assistance dog.

🐾 Take your list, review it independently and with family and friends to get open, honest feedback on what you have put in each column of your list. Do the positives outweigh the negatives? If so, keep reading to determine the next steps to take.

Part 3

So, you believe an assistance dog is the right tool for you. Now what?

So, you're convinced an assistance dog will help you mitigate the effects of your disability, will fit into your lifestyle, and that you will be able to properly care for them, ultimately creating a mutually beneficial partnership. Great! The last step is to determine—of the two main avenues—what method of getting and working with an assistance dog is best for you.

One method is to get a dog on your own and train it yourself or with the help of a professional trainer. At a growing rate, people are successfully training their own assistance dog and this avenue is becoming more popular. The second method is to go through a professional assistance dog organization that will match you with one of their trained assistance dogs that can provide skills that mitigate your specific disability. Historically, this is the most common, and it's typically considered the easiest process.

Both are valid avenues to get to the same goal. However, they are very different in your required tolerance for an untrained dog and the variability in success rates. I will discuss both factors in more detail, including common reasons why dogs may not be successful as assistance dogs. Then we will discuss considerations for choosing an assistance dog organization or a trainer to work with. As they employ different methods, it's important to do your homework so you can choose the one that will best suit you, making it more likely you will be as successful as possible throughout this journey.

I have worked in various capacities with large and small assistance dog organizations, as well as with people who have trained their own assistance dogs. I have seen successes and failures from each method, as they each have their benefits and challenges. I can assure you that if you seriously consider which method will work best for you before jumping in, you will be more successful. If you skip this section and choose a method that isn't right for you, then—no matter how hard you try or how good your intentions are—the probability of your being successful with your assistance dog will decrease dramatically.

Part 3 learning objectives

By the end of reading Part 3, you will be able to...

- determine which avenue of training is most likely to lead to success for you.
- recognize why not all dogs want to be assistance dogs.
- identify the pros and cons for each training avenue.
- determine how to choose the right assistance dog organization or trainer for your needs.

Note: assistance dog organizations, from here on out, will be called organizations.

CHAPTER 11

Considerations for what training stage you begin with

There are two main avenues to getting an assistance dog. Neither is better nor worse; they are just different methods to get to the same goal. Neither is an easy process, and both will take considerable time, effort, patience, resiliency, and consistency on your part. However, depending on your abilities and disabilities, one avenue may lead to a higher chance of success than the other.

This chapter will describe the differences in the methods, enabling you to make an educated decision on which avenue is best for you. Throughout this chapter, take an honest and objective look at your capabilities to determine which method has a higher chance of leading to success for you.

Getting a dog that is *not* already trained

The first avenue involves getting a dog that is *not* already trained for assistance work, with the intention of training it yourself.

This avenue will involve a lot of training on your part before the dog can be considered an assistance dog. During this initial period of training, the dog will be considered an "assistance dog in training." Once you, as the handler, feel that your dog is reliable in their skills that mitigate your disability in many settings and consistently displays appropriate behavior at home and in public, then they can be labeled "an assistance dog."

If you decide to train your own dog, the time you expend should begin much younger in the dog's life than if you get an assistance dog from an organization. All successful assistance dogs go through all training stages from puppyhood, basic socialization and obedience, public-access training, to training specific skills that can mitigate their handler's disability.

If you intend to train your own dog, intentional training should begin from the moment you acquire the dog. These dogs are typically acquired from a breeder, rescue organization, or shelter. More important than where the dog is acquired is the dog's age. Younger dogs tend to be more successful than dogs who start training when they are older. The older the dog is when it starts this process, the more challenges you may experience.

The earlier you can expose a dog to various environments the better, as every assistance dog needs to be comfortable and confident in different public environments. Young dogs go through fear periods, and if they are not exposed to things during this time that they will be exposed to throughout their life, they may become fearful of them. Therefore, the later you begin the process of training the dog intentionally for assistance work, the more challenges you are likely to encounter.

Consequently, undesirable fears or behaviors may have already become ingrained, which will make it harder, but not necessarily impossible, to correct any unwanted behaviors.

Every assistance dog also needs to be under the handler's control in public and behave appropriately. This involves walking nicely next to the handler, not interacting with the public, being unobtrusive, not relieving themselves in public, not barking excessively, etc. As just mentioned, if an assistance dog is behaving inappropriately, disturbing others, a shop owner does have the right to ask you to remove your dog.

Training appropriate behavior in public often begins with a strong foundation in basic obedience. Although this is not required, it helps ensure that you can control your dog in various situations. Similarly, it is not required to hire a professional dog trainer to assist you. However, dog trainers are commonly utilized in training one's own assistance dog, and I encourage you to use a few different dog trainers, as they have different perspectives and can provide different training tips, especially if they don't have experience training assistance dogs. Commonly, people will work with a dog trainer during puppy socialization classes, basic obedience classes, Canine Good Citizen classes, or other classes related to their skill work.

You cannot expect that just by working with a professional dog trainer, your dog will become an assistance dog. You will need to put in significant effort at times when you are not physically with the trainer, as the trainer will be present only a small fraction of the time you are training your dog. Everything your dog does, especially when young, can be a training opportunity, either to reward the dog for a behavior that you want to continue, ignoring behavior that you want to extinguish, or redirecting the dog to more appropriate behaviors. If you expect that just by working with a dog trainer once per week your dog will be an assistance dog, this is not the method for you.

One benefit of training your own dog is that you have a lot more involvement and control over the training process. This is beneficial, as you can name behaviors and skills that make the most sense to you. Whereas if you get a dog from an organization, they use certain cue words you will need to learn.

Although you have more control over the initial training, there is no guarantee that your dog will enjoy the training or be successful with it. Therefore, the main downside of training your own assistance dog is that there is less of a guarantee your dog will want to be an assistance dog, that it will have the temperament to be an assistance dog or the skills to reliably be an assistance dog. This uncertainty is important to consider when choosing which avenue is best for you.

Mary spent four years diligently training a shelter puppy named Summer to become her assistance dog. Due to her disability being variable and still trying to hold a full-time job, Mary was unable to train Summer as much as she would have liked when the dog was young. She found that taking Summer out as a puppy was exhausting; even short outings would wipe her out for the rest of the day. Although she hired a great trainer, Mary found it very difficult to be consistent in her training over time due to the variable nature of her disability and the amount of time and energy Summer required. The upshot was that long-term, Summer was not very comfortable in public, and even after four years of training classes, she could perform a few disability-mitigating skills but had not learned to be reliable in performing them. This was not beneficial to Mary, as she could not, especially in public, count on Summer to consistently complete the needed work.

Although Mary was determined and gave it a lot of effort, she was unsuccessful. It may be different for you. But carefully and realistically consider your ability to do the training *consistently from puppyhood*. Having no assistance dog at all is better than a poorly trained assistance dog that is unreliable at mitigating the effects of your disability. If you know you will not be consistent or patient in the training, this avenue is not recommended for you.

🐾 How tolerant would you be in training an untrained dog?

🐾 How tolerant would you be in working through the puppy period?

Getting a dog that is already trained

The second avenue is to get a dog that is already trained. These dogs typically come from a professional organization whose sole purpose is to raise, train, and place assistance dogs for people with disabilities. There are also individual dog trainers not associated with an organization that offer this service. When acquiring a dog that is already trained, there is typically a very short period where the dog is still considered "in training" before it becomes an assistance dog.

Typically, this "in training" stage occurs while you, the handler, learn to work with the dog. If you choose this method, most of the learning will be done by you, learning to successfully work with the dog in the way the dog knows how to work. Therefore, you are learning what the dog already knows.

This is not to say that you won't be doing any training. You will be training your dog to work with *you*, and irrespective of what stage you begin training with a dog, the dog will require maintenance training for life, as emphasized previously. However, this avenue doesn't require tolerance for the puppy stage or for working with an untrained dog. This is because where you enter the process begins at a much later stage in the dog's life, as it bypasses the puppy period and working with an untrained dog.

Even if you choose to work with an already-trained dog from an organization, there is no guarantee that you and your dog will make a successful assistance dog team. For example, after working together it could be decided that the match is not appropriate based on lifestyle, incompatibility in personalities, energy levels, stress levels, or other factors. However, the chances of success are significantly higher because the dog has already been vetted to be good in public, well trained, and has mastered the skills you need. Additionally, organizations take great care and consideration in their matching process.

Each organization has different techniques and processes for teaching their clients to work with their matched assistance dog. If you believe this to be the best avenue for you, you must choose an organization that will work best for you. Chapter 13 will walk you through considerations for choosing the right organization (or trainer).

In general, an organization that trains assistance dogs will intensively work with you initially to teach you everything you need to know about working with an assistance dog successfully. This training will begin before your dog moves home with you and should continue afterwards to ensure you have a successful transition to working with the dog in your home.

Overall, your tolerance for the initial untrained stage is the main differing factor between the two avenues. The good thing is, as a handler, unless you want to, you do not have to participate in *every* stage of training. If you want to receive a fully trained assistance dog from an organization, it's possible. If you want to raise a puppy into a fully trained assistance dog, that's also possible. For both methods, you will need to devote a lot of time, effort, patience, resiliency, and consistency to the process, or you will not be successful. These factors will be discussed next.

Time

Irrespective of the avenue you choose, once you start working with a dog and you two are a successful team, you will need to devote a significant portion of your time to that dog for their entire life. After all, the dog is part of your life, and caring for them and maintaining their training will be time demanding.

The difference between the two avenues is the length of time during which you don't have a relative guarantee you will be a successful team. People who choose to train their own dog will devote much more time working with their dog *before* it is clear whether the dog will make it as an assistance dog or not. People who choose to get an already-trained dog will typically know much sooner whether their partnership with the assistance dog will be successful. The difference in this could be two years, possibly more.

Often assistance dogs are not able to be considered fully trained until at minimum eighteen months to two years of age (or more). This is because they are still developing and maturing throughout the second year. Therefore, a person who gets a dog as a puppy may not know until two years later whether the dog wants to be an assistance dog or has what it takes to be an assistance dog. Comparatively, people who get an already-trained dog can typically tell within a couple of months if they will be successful together.

Although unfortunate, just because you put the time in, it doesn't assure a successful outcome. This is because some dogs just don't want to be an assistance dog, and that's okay. I will discuss this in Chapter 12.

If you choose to get an already-trained dog, your time involved in working with an assistance dog *before* it's fully trained is minimal. However, you could still have devoted a lot of passive time to the process, as many organizations require an application, interview and have a long waitlist. Therefore, the time spent waiting before working with an assistance dog successfully may be similar in length to those who choose to train their own dog, yet the effort expended during this time is minimal compared to when training one's own assistance dog.

🐾 How much time do you want to or can commit to working with a dog before they may or may not be considered an assistance dog?

Effort

Once working with a dog with the intent that they'll be an assistance dog, regardless of the avenue you took to get there, you will be expending similar amounts of effort to work with your dog and maintain their training for life.

Training your own assistance dog will take significantly more effort initially. The discrepancy in effort is due to all the initial training, involving socialization, basic obedience, and skill work that handlers of already-trained assistance dogs don't need to do. It takes a *lot* of effort to train a puppy or dog. The puppy period alone is very tiring, even for healthy, able-bodied people.

Professional trainers work forty-plus hours per week, training dogs to become assistance dogs. And it's not a given, even so, that their dogs will successfully reach that goal. I'm not saying that *because* professional trainers can't always do it, you can't either. That's not true. I say this to emphasize that you can put all the effort in the world into training your own dog, and still there's a chance the dog will not make the cut. If a dog chooses not to want to be an assistance dog, you need to respect that choice to be a companion dog instead.

Seriously consider whether you can respect the dog's choice to be a pet if your dog is showing you that preference. If not, then an assistance dog is not the right choice for you. As a handler, you always need to keep your dog's best interests in mind. Any dog that doesn't like assistance dog work should never be forced into that role.

People who get an already-trained dog start working with a basically fully trained assistance dog. Therefore, the effort they put into the initial training before it becomes a fully trained assistance dog is significantly less than that of people who train their own dog. Seriously consider if you are willing to put in the effort upfront to train an assistance dog even if it might not work out.

🐾 How much effort can you commit to working with a dog before they may or may not be considered an assistance dog?

Patience

Once working with a dog, any dog, but especially with the intent for it to be highly trained, you will need a lot of patience. Dogs make mistakes, and working through these mistakes will require patience, especially as you learn to work together. This is true irrespective of which avenue you choose.

However, just based on trials and tribulations common with raising a puppy, those who train their own dog will need *even more patience* than those who get an already-trained assistance dog.

Puppies are hard work! Initially it's a lot like having a newborn. They will wake you up in the middle of the night; they will have accidents in the house; they may cry or bark and sleep a lot. Are you able to handle the initial puppy stages while also taking care of yourself? Remember, you are creating a mutually beneficial relationship; you should not be sacrificing your health and safety for the addition of a puppy into your life.

Even a fully trained assistance dog is a lot like a three-year-old human. They will have energy; they will make mistakes, and they will act silly. Do you have the patience for a three-year-old living with you?

🐾 Do you have the patience to work with a dog during the puppy period or the very much untrained stage?

🐾 Do you have patience for a dog who will act like a dog and not be perfect all the time?

Resiliency

Resiliency is also an important quality to have as an assistance dog handler. Things will not be perfect, and training will be challenging. After all, assistance dogs are not robots or magical unicorns. They are animals who will push your buttons irrespective of what stage of training they are in.

Especially if you plan to train your own assistance dog, there will be days where you get knocked off course and want to quit, or where your dog is doing things and you don't know why, or you know your dog knows something and they aren't able to perform it for whatever reason, etc. Therefore, being resilient, able to step back, look at the big picture, then get yourself back on course, will be helpful. This will further be beneficial, as working with an assistance dog is a journey that won't happen overnight.

You can expect to experience setbacks, so all assistance dog handlers need to be resilient. You and your dog will make mistakes, and some of these will occur in public. If you are not resilient, especially in public, it will be harder to overcome these training challenges. If you can move on from your mistakes in a positive way, you will be more successful. Therefore, it's important to be resilient and not put too much pressure on yourself or the dog to succeed. If there is too much pressure and not enough resilience, the team is more likely to fail.

🐾 Are you resilient enough to bounce back from mistakes? Even ones that occur in public?

Consistency

Consistency is important for all dogs and is a big part of training or maintaining training as dogs thrive on consistency. If you are not consistent in what you ask of your dog or how you respond to your dog when they do certain things, the dog will not learn or understand what the rules or expectations are. Without consistency, the dog will become confused and have a harder time learning what is expected of them and what is inappropriate. This is important to ensure your dog behaves properly in public and is consistent in their skills. Therefore, it is important in dog training, whether that be from a puppy or even as a dog you get fully trained, to be consistent in the rules you set and what behaviors you will and will not tolerate. Without rules and consistency, your well-trained dog will regress back to an untrained dog.

🐾 Are you able to be consistent with a dog?

Dog experience

To work with an assistance dog, all the above factors are necessary. What is not necessary is having dog experience. I have worked with many people who have never lived with a dog or had much experience with dogs yet are successful with an assistance dog.

However, your level of dog experience is important to consider when deciding what avenue is right for you. If you don't have *any* dog experience, you will probably be more successful if you get an assistance dog that is already trained. This is primarily because of the volume of new information you would need to acquire, and practically master, in a short period while dealing with a lot of internal and external pressure on you and your dog. This is typically not realistic.

The more dog experience you have, especially firsthand experience working with dogs, the easier this process will be overall. If you have lived with multiple dogs, or better yet trained multiple dogs at least to basic obedience standards, your chances of success in training an assistance dog will increase. However, general experience with dogs is different from the functional experience of working with a dog.

Generally, being around dogs and growing up with dogs doesn't necessarily mean that you know how to work with a dog, read their body language, or be able to communicate with a dog. None of these skills are necessary (though they are beneficial) for having a companion dog; they are, however, essential in having an assistance dog.

When working with an assistance dog, it is important to understand dog behavior, read dog body language and be able to effectively respond to and communicate with a dog. This is not a skill set acquired just by having lived with a dog. Many companion dog owners are limited in their ability to successfully read their dog's body language and often can't tell when their dog is stressed or overwhelmed. The better you are at understanding dogs and in responding accordingly, the more successful you will be in training a dog to become an assistance dog or working with an assistance dog in general.

It is not enough to understand dogs; you also need to communicate what you need from them in a clear way. If you are unclear in your training or cues, your dog will have a more difficult time understanding what you want. This will be challenging, as dogs typically want to please, but if they don't know what you want, it can be frustrating for both parties involved.

Out of all these factors, dog experience is the least important to have currently, as it can be learned through getting a dog, attending dog-training classes, reading books, watching videos, and surrounding yourself with knowledgeable people. Having and gaining dog experience will make the process a bit easier; however, it will still be much more difficult than raising a companion dog.

Overall, if you choose to raise and train your own dog to become your assistance dog, this will be a much more challenging process and may incur a lower success rate than getting an assistance dog from an organization. However, when successful, it is incredibly empowering and fulfilling.

The hard truth is, irrespective of disability, some people are capable of raising a puppy into a fully trained assistance dog and some are not. Even for healthy, able-bodied people, raising a well-adjusted, successful dog is challenging. It is a difficult process that not every person can accomplish. However, if you can devote the time, put in the effort, learn to read and communicate with your dog, are resilient and consistent, you will be more successful than individuals without these qualities.

If these qualities describe you, you will have a higher chance of success training and working with an assistance dog in general than if you lacked these qualities. If these qualities don't describe you, I'm not saying you won't be successful with an assistance dog, just that being successful will take even more effort and will probably involve more assistance from your social support network.

🐾 Which of these factors (time, effort, patience, resiliency, consistency) come naturally to you, and which ones would you struggle with more?

🐾 How could you work to increase your ability in the factors that you would struggle with?

CHAPTER 12

Considerations for your dog's success

Before working with an assistance dog, it's important to know both what factors indicate that a dog should not become an assistance dog and, secondly, what the general success rate of becoming an assistance dog is.

Obviously, as is well known, not all dogs want to be an assistance dog, and that's okay! In fact, of all the dogs in the world, only a very small proportion have what it takes to complete training and be comfortable with all that is required of an assistance dog.

Assistance dogs need to have the desire to do the work, and specifically the work that you need them to do. Some dogs want to be medical alert dogs and use their nose, while others enjoy alerting to sounds, yet others are more interested in doing physical things or snuggling with their person. Therefore, you need to carefully consider what specialty a particular dog wants to spend their life doing and whether this matches the work you need them to do. This is especially important to consider if you are training your own dog, as unless they want to do the type of work you need done, they won't be successful.

It can also happen that throughout the training period, a dog seems perfectly satisfied with being an assistance dog—successful at it—but nevertheless in the end decides against it. This may occur even after dogs are working with the handler they were matched with by an organization. In that case, we need to accept the dog's decision. The dog is at that point considered "career changed." Commonly, a dog is career changed to become a companion dog, or if the dog likes working but is not congenial with assistance dog work, the new career might be as a therapy dog, detection dog, or other type of working dog. Even if your dog rejects assistance dog work, don't think you as a person have failed!

The reasons why an assistance dog may be career changed are manifold.

They don't have the desire to work

Some dogs just don't have the desire to work. Just like I don't have the desire to be an accountant, your dog may not have the desire for assistance dog work. Do not make a dog who doesn't have the desire to work, work. If you insist, you will not be a successful team, and your relationship will be strained in the long run.

In your life you have free will regarding a career; no one is forcing you (not even your parents) to be an accountant when you want to be something else. If you were forced to be an accountant, you would probably dread your job and not do your work well. The same is true for dogs. Some like assistance dog work; some want to work in search and rescue; some in herding other animals; and some prefer the companion dog lifestyle.

If you push a dog into a role that they aren't happy in, you will be fighting an uphill battle for the rest of your partnership.

Additionally, a dog that doesn't have the desire to work will not be reliable. An assistance dog who is not reliable is just a dog that can do tricks. Reliability for assistance dogs can mean life or death for the handler. Therefore, you need an assistance dog to be reliable in performing their skills, which they cannot do if they don't want to work.

If they don't have the desire to do the work that you need, there may be another person or organization out there who does need your dog for the work the dog enjoys. Organizations are good at networking, for this reason, and have connections with each other to give dogs the ability to live the career they feel best suited to.

If your dog doesn't have the desire to be an assistance dog, you must be comfortable letting them be career changed.

They are not comfortable in public

Not every human is comfortable in every setting, and this is the same for dogs. I, for example, am not comfortable on boats. If I had a job where I needed to work on a boat, I would be miserable; I would dread going to work. Thankfully, I can decline a job that would require me to work on a boat. However, for dogs, this option is not available. A dog is on a leash with you and, therefore, must go where you take them.

Consequently, it is incredibly important that you can read your dog's body language, identifying what things or situations make your dog uncomfortable. If, for example, your dog is not comfortable going in public, let alone having to do a job in public, the quality of their work, if they are even able to perform their job at all, will be poor. Do not make a dog who is uncomfortable in public settings work in public or go out in public. It is up to you, as a good dog handler, to take the dog's preferences into consideration and not bring the dog into situations that make them uncomfortable or where they are nervous to be.

These dogs can still be great at working; however, they are just not comfortable in public. Therefore, they could be wonderful, skilled companions at home, where they can do work or trained tasks in a comfortable environment. They should not, though, be asked to go in public and especially work in public if it is stressful for them. As discussed in Chapter 7, some organizations match these types of dogs as well, giving them a range of names, including "skilled home companions."

If your dog is not comfortable in public, they should be career changed or given a job where they don't have to work in public.

They get stressed when too much is asked of them

Just like I would get stressed in a high-stakes medical job, some dogs get stressed when too much is asked of them. This can be true even if they physically can do the job. Though I do not doubt my ability to learn the information and skills needed to work in the medical environment, I know that due to the stress and pressure I would be under, I would not be a good surgeon. In this situation, I would not enjoy my job and would probably shut down when it came time to perform surgery.

Dogs are similar. Just because in the quiet environment of your home they can be taught a skill doesn't mean they will be able to perform that skill in a busy mall environment, or if there is a pressure of "I need this now," which is often the case in emergencies, where you may need help immediately.

This pressure will not preclude some dogs from working. Depending on the severity of the stress, the ability of the handler to read the dog's stress signs, and the handler's ability to relieve the stress, the dog may or may not be able to work through this stress. If the stress is too much for the dog, it can break their desire to work at all, in which case the dog should be career changed.

Even assistance dog organizations may not realize the level of stress a dog may feel, moving into the handler's home and life, compared to the stress levels the organization's trainers saw the dog experience during training. A handler's home is a completely new environment, with a different and potentially more stressful workload. This is often caused by being expected to be available to the handler for more time than they ever have before, which can be too much for some dogs. This could affect the dog's ability to work and wouldn't be something that the organization could predict.

If your dog becomes overly stressed when too much is asked of them, it's time to career change them.

They are not physically fit to work

Another valid reason for being career changed is physical fitness. Some dogs are not fit enough physically to be capable of doing the work we want them to. Before finalizing the training of an assistance dog, it's important to make sure to test the health of the dog—with all the relevant medical clearances having been passed. This typically includes checking the hips and elbows to make sure they don't have (or are prone to) dysplasia. Often, skills that are asked of an assistance dog could put extra strain on these joints, and if they are not properly structured, it could decrease the dog's overall quality of life, especially if asked to work with these abnormalities.

Based on physical or genetic weaknesses common to the breed, there may be other health clearances to check. A veterinarian should clear your dog for these before working. The more of these problems you can circumvent by selecting good breeding and testing, when appropriate, the more you will help the dog be able to do their job for as long as possible.

If your dog is not physically fit to do work, they should be career changed.

Irrespective of the avenue you choose to get an assistance dog through, you always need to have the dog's best interests in mind. Don't put the skills, trainability, or temperament of the dog over the dog's health, comfort, or desire to do what you need them to do as an assistance dog. As a responsible assistance dog handler, this is the most important thing you can do to help your dog have a long and healthy career.

Success rates

It is impossible to determine whether a dog will be successful as an assistance dog before they begin training. This is true even for dogs who have been specifically bred for many generations to work as an assistance dog.

Often large (and even small) organizations have their own breeding program and are part of an international collaboration focused on breeding assistance dogs. This international collaboration was designed to produce the best assistance dogs possible. Even with this goal in mind, continual research and best practices implemented, not every dog they produce wants to be an assistance dog. These organizations also employ professional trainers, yet often only have a 50 to 70 percent success rate of the dogs that pass through their program. Therefore, the success rate of any ol' dog from the shelter, rescue, or breeder is likely to be even lower.

By going through an organization, you know that the dog has already been vetted to be well-trained, comfortable in public, healthy, and they can perform the skills you need. The probability of success with your assistance dog is therefore higher. Even then, however, the success rate is not 100 percent. This is because an organization or trainer cannot definitively guarantee that once a dog is placed with a handler, they will embrace being an assistance dog as a full-time career, nor can you guarantee that other unexpected behavioral or health conditions won't arise.

Raising and training a dog on your own has a much lower success rate because there is no guarantee that your dog will have the abilities, desire, or comfort in public to be your assistance dog. If your dog, in the end, doesn't enjoy or isn't comfortable with assistance dog work, then you have potentially invested a lot of time, energy, and money into a well-trained companion dog, which is great, but not what you need to help mitigate your disability.

If at any time throughout the process of raising or training your assistance dog, they demonstrate being unhappy in an assistance dog role, you need to respect this decision and career change them.

Therefore, it is important to consider now what you would do if you had a dog who decided not to be an assistance dog. If you got the dog through an organization, the organization should take the dog back and find them a new, appropriate home. However, if you are considering training your own dog, you need to think carefully, in advance, about how you would proceed. Can you physically and financially keep the career-changed dog with you if you want to attempt to train another dog? Or will you need to rehome them?

🐾 If you decide to train your own dog and that dog decides against the assistance dog lifestyle—that it's not the life they want—what will you do with the dog? Be specific.

CHAPTER 13

Considerations when vetting an organization or a trainer

Irrespective of whether you get an assistance dog from an organization or train one yourself with the help of a dog trainer, verify that you are working with the right person or organization, one committed to helping you accomplish your goals in a way that works for you. Not all organizations or dog trainers are created equal. Consequently, you will need to vet the organization or trainer. To do this, make sure of these six things:

1. The quality of the dogs they produce is high.
2. You can financially afford them.
3. Their training method is a good fit for you.
4. Their training location and type are a good fit for you.
5. You can communicate with them.
6. That they have your best interests in mind.

I will discuss each of these in turn.

Quality

Whether you plan to work with an organization or a trainer, make sure the quality of dogs they produce is high. The quality of assistance dogs can vary, based on the assistance dog organization or the experience of the trainer. Therefore, you will want to assess their product, experience, and credentials.

Can their dogs do what they advertise? It is important that their dogs can do what they say and that they can do it reliably, over their lifetime. To determine this, watch a demonstration of their dogs, if possible, whether in person or through videos. It can also be beneficial to chat with current or past clients or read their testimonials.

What is their experience in training assistance dogs? How many assistance dogs have they successfully trained? Will your dog be the first or their one hundredth successful assistance dog? Make sure you are going with an experienced organization or trainer. Otherwise, your opportunity for success will likely be lower.

What is their experience in working with people with disabilities? What about your disability specifically or something similar? Just because a person can train dogs doesn't mean that that person is successful working with people, let alone people with various disabilities. To be as successful as possible, make sure the trainer has experience working with people with disabilities similar to yours and is capable of adapting the training, as needed, to accommodate you.

What is the trainer's definition of a successful assistance dog team? Does it involve a belief that any dog can work with any person? This is not true and is a red flag. Do the trainer's dogs have long-term success as assistance dogs, or do they fall apart after a few months/years of partnership? Another red flag. It is important to work with someone who is committed to your success as a team for the lifetime of your working relationship, not just initially. You will want to work with someone you can come back to, over and over, to answer your questions and help you when challenges arise, working through them with you.

Therefore, do your research to choose the best organization or trainer you can.

If you are interested in working with an organization, the vetting process can be a little bit easier. The best way to determine if the organization you are interested in produces high-quality dogs is to verify them with Assistance Dogs International (ADI) or the International Guide Dog Federation (IGDF). These are both international overseeing accrediting bodies of organizations. Each organization they accredit has gone through a rigorous process to ensure the quality of the dogs they produce is up to their high standard and that they have a commitment to their handlers for the life of the dog.

ADI and IGDF are there to protect you as a client of the organization. They have rigorously vetted each organization so that you know they are not a scam, and you can be certain of their ability and quality of work. They also stay up to date on the latest research and implement current best practices for each type of assistance dog. They are continually trying to improve the assistance dog industry so the dogs can be the best that they can be, for you and the dogs.

Organizations that are not accredited by ADI or IGDF may produce just as high-quality dogs. However, there is less guarantee. Especially, avoid organizations or trainers that cost a lot of money upfront and do minimal follow-up training with you.

Cost

The upfront cost of getting an assistance dog can vary widely—ranging from many thousands of dollars to free. Currently, the generally agreed-upon estimated cost for an assistance dog is forty-five thousand US dollars. Some people estimate the cost to be higher. A dog provided to a handler free of charge is not valued any less than an expensive dog. Rather, the difference comes from the way the organization or trainer acquires their funds.

Dog trainers typically charge hourly rates for their services. Organizations, on the other hand, typically have a flat rate for their dogs. Typically, you need to pay this upfront before you start working with an assistance dog or possibly before you are even placed on a waitlist.

Alternatively, some organizations provide assistance dogs free of charge to people who meet their requirements. By receiving grants or relying on generous donors to fund the care and training of the dogs initially, these organizations are typically able to forego putting this cost on the handler. Sometimes, the organizations will still charge an application fee, typically less than one hundred dollars.

Irrespective of the upfront cost, you will still need to financially afford the dog's care. We went over this in depth in Chapter 6. You must consider whether you can financially afford the price tag for the organization or trainer you are interested in working with, plus the cost of care for the life of the dog.

Either way you go, make sure to evaluate your organization or your trainer to ascertain where your money will be spent and the likelihood of you getting a high-quality assistance dog. You don't want to be the next horror story of a person who pays many thousands of dollars to an organization or dog trainer who claims to provide assistance dogs, only to find out, not long afterwards, that you were given a well-trained companion dog who doesn't have the skills to mitigate your disability and/ or doesn't have an ability to be in public. Such dogs may be able to do a few things for you, but typically they are unable to provide the full support you need or are unreliable.

In these situations, the organization or trainer is also typically difficult to contact afterward for follow-up assistance. By all means, avoid these organizations or trainers.

Training method

Within dog training as a whole, not just for assistance dogs, there are various styles or methods of training. There is no one singular method that all dog trainers or organizations use. Rather, the methods are a somewhat contentious topic within the industry, with many opinions on what the "right" methods for dog training are. Therefore, do your research on what methods you agree with or don't.

Common training methods are briefly described below.

Positive reinforcement is one of the most popular training methods, as it is based on rewarding the behaviors that you want to continue (such as giving a treat when the dog sits) and ignoring those that you do not want. These techniques are well supported by science to be positive for both the dog and handler and to be effective.

Negative punishment involves removing a desired thing (such as your shoe) if the dog does an undesired behavior (eating your shoe). There is no real "punishment" here; simply, something the dog likes is taken away. This allows the dog to try again and perform a behavior that you approve of (such as chewing a bone instead).

Positive punishment involves the addition of something the dog deems undesirable (such as being hit for jumping on you). Other positive punishment includes using an electric collar, a prong collar, or spraying the dog with a water bottle. These and other tools have a specific purpose in dog training and should be used *with expert guidance only*. This method is less preferable, in general, as it has the potential to ruin your relationship with your dog.

Negative reinforcement is also typically not desirable, as it involves *removing* a painful or unpleasant experience for the dog (that you typically inflict), once the desired behavior is performed. For example, this could be pinning a dog to the ground until they stop trying to bite your hand. Such an action can instill fear of you and can also ruin your relationship with your dog.

Alpha, or dominance-type training has decreased its popularity in recent years, as science has found it to be unfounded, problematic, and dangerous. It often relies on the handler being the "pack leader" and enforcing positive punishment to maintain that status. I do not recommend utilizing a trainer or organization that relies on this method.

Relationship-based training emphasizes your relationship with your dog and aims to keep the training positive, and not stressful, by moving at a pace and in a style that works for your dog. This method requires you to be able to read and understand dog body language and communication well.

Clicker training is a type of positive reinforcement that uses a clicker tool that produces a "click" noise to more immediately indicate to the dog that what they did was correct and a reward is coming. A marker word like "yes" can also be used in place of the clicker sound. This is a common method used by organizations.

Each trainer or organization is free to use more than one of these (or other) training methods. The method employed may depend on the situation or what the dog responds to best.

When determining whom you want to work with, make sure you are comfortable using the methods that they use. Most commonly, this applies to trainers who use positive punishment, negative reinforcement, or alpha/dominance. Are you comfortable giving your dog physical corrections if they did something wrong? Are you okay with using various pieces of equipment that may be recommended, such as prong collars or e-collars? Are you physically able to use a clicker? If not, make sure to choose an organization that uses training methods or equipment you are comfortable with.

🐾 Do your research. What types of training are you comfortable with?

Training location and strategy

Dog trainers and organizations also have different training *strategies* for working with their clients.

Typically, dog trainers train one-on-one. Initially, you may be encouraged to attend group classes—for example, for the puppy stage and to gain basic obedience. Once your dog is advanced enough in basic skills to start working on specific assistance dog skills to mitigate your disability, they typically encourage individual training sessions. Dog trainers may have very flexible time availability or not, depending on their workload with other clients. In general, dog trainers are busy people with a full workload. Therefore, it may be up to you to be flexible as to when and where you train with them.

Organizations have various methods for teaching clients to work with their dogs. Therefore, you must make sure the organization's methods will be appropriate for you and how you best learn. For example, some organizations teach clients to work with their dogs in group settings, with at least two clients learning to work with their dogs at the same time, while others only teach one-on-one. Additionally, some organizations only teach at their facility, while others come to your home and community or a combination of both.

Group training is beneficial because handlers can learn from each other. Even if their disabilities are not similar, it is beneficial for handlers to see other handlers and dogs who are at the same stage in their partnership. This allows you to see other teams' successes and struggles, which may be similar to or different from what you are going through. However, when you see the challenges that you watched someone else experience in training, now in your own relationship down the road, you will be better equipped to handle the situation. Group training is also a great way to form relationships with other handlers who are going through similar situations so you can lean on each other for support now and in the future.

The downside of group training is that the lessons are typically *one size fits all*. This can cause challenges when the speed of clients' progression is dissimilar. Handlers can become frustrated or discouraged if they feel they are holding up the class, while others, progressing faster than the class, may feel bored. Managing this dynamic is the trainer's responsibility.

Other times, organizations do individual training. This is a great method if you need more one-on-one attention or a slower or more accelerated pace. The downside to individual training is the lack of social support from other handlers. Not having this support and first-hand validation that everyone experiences challenges working with their dog in the beginning can make them feel more alone in the process.

The location of training is also important to consider. How close or far is the trainer or organization from your home? Is it a car ride, road trip, or plane trip away? The closer the location is to you in general, the easier it will be for all parties involved due to the convenience of proximity.

Organizations typically start training at their facility because the dog is familiar with their facility, and it is convenient initially for them. The benefit of starting training at the facility is that only one of you is in a new location learning new things. By this, I mean that the dog will be comfortable working at the training facility where they practiced and mastered their skills. However, you are new to the facility and to working with a dog. This means that you are more likely to make mistakes than your dog is. This should be expected and is strategic.

Since only one of you is in a new situation, you are setting yourself up for greater success than if both of you were in a new situation, the dog in a new home and you working with the dog for the first time. Therefore, working at the facility initially is typically preferred by organizations, as there are fewer new variables interfering in the training process.

The knowledge you gain initially from working at the facility can then be translated when you go back home and start working with the dog there and in your community because now you are more experienced as a handler and can manage situations when your dog makes a mistake because of being in a new environment.

Further along in your partnership, organizations may switch their training to your home and community. Even later, the organization may request that if you have challenges with your dog along your journey or want follow-up training, you come back to their facility, although some will come to your home.

Irrespective of what type of training setting you feel is best, make sure that your trainer or organization offers continuing training and assistance for the lifetime of your dog. As should be expected, you will run into challenges, and you want someone you can reach out to for help, relying on your organization or trainer to assist you throughout the working life of the dog. This is a requirement for ADI and IGDF accredited organizations.

Communication

Communication is a two-way street. Make sure you assess the organization or trainer as open and honest in their communication with you. You also need to be very open and honest with the organization or trainer. Initially, both parties' goal should be to make sure the facilitator is the right entity to assist you to reach your goal of working with an assistance dog.

Before you start working with an organization or trainer, you may undergo an interview process. This is incredibly important for both parties to get information about the other. The provider will ask detailed questions to determine if they are the right entity to assist you in managing your disability with the help of an assistance dog and whether they can provide you with what you need in a way that will make you successful.

During the interview, you should be asking similar questions of the organization or trainer to make sure that they are the right entity for you as well.

To make this decision, and subsequent decisions in the future, the organization will need to know a lot of personal information. This will include not only information about your disability and how it impacts your daily life, but also things like how you deal with stress or challenges, what your house is like, details about what your day entails, etc. You may think that much of this information is irrelevant, like how many stairs you have to climb to get into your house or what type of neighbors you have. Even these mundane aspects are important information for them to understand you and your life so they can set you up for success when matching you with or teaching you to work with an assistance dog.

After all, assistance dogs are a piece of medical equipment, and they are incredibly valuable because they can be tailored to each handler. The trainers (especially those from organizations) are the experts on this form of medical equipment, and they know how to calibrate the dog to each person. Since each dog is different, with unique quirks and preferences, it can be a delicate process of matching and of teaching a person to work with the dog.

Assistance dog trainers are the experts on assistance dogs, but you are the expert of you. Therefore, you need to be open and honest with your trainer and the two of you work together to assist them in calibrating the dog to your needs. Beyond just fitting the dog to assist with your disability-mitigating needs (retrieves, alerts, guiding, etc.), during training the trainers are also equipping you with tools and resources on how to work with your specific dog. They are assisting you in building a full toolbox that you can turn to and rely on in various situations during initial training and in the future.

Some of the tools they are equipping you with may include what to do when certain medical conditions flare up, even if they are not present during the interview or training. Therefore, the trainer needs to know about *all* your medical conditions. Otherwise, the trainer may not know to provide the tools you need now or will in the future to work with your dog successfully.

A condition or challenge that you experience may, to the untrained eye, seem insignificant. However, this information is important to the trainer because I guarantee you that the trainers are training you and your dog far more than you realize during the initial phase. If they do their job well, there may never be a time that you realize those extra bits of training that went into it because the problems down the road didn't arise, or you have the tools necessary to work through the problems on your own. This is only successful when the trainers know the full extent of what they can expect when working with you and what the dog can expect when living with you.

Therefore, the trainer's goal in knowing your medical condition and what may seem like insignificant pieces of information about your life or condition is to allow them to give you more or different tools for your toolbox, as everyone's toolbox is unique to them and their dog.

Some of these tools may not be necessary now but may be in the future if conditions get worse or change. Then you would already have the resources to deal with the situation. No one can know everything that will happen in the future with a medical condition or new conditions arising, but the trainers can try to set you up for the best possible success with the information that is available at the time of training.

By working with a trainer or organization, you are getting the benefit of their years of collective experience. In general, assistance dog trainers are passionate about what they do, and they work in this industry because they want to help you be as successful as possible working with your assistance dog. Assuming you found an organization or trainer that is passionate about helping you, rather than the money, trust them in their decision-making process and the rules they set. They are the experts. After all, you are working with them for a reason.

Throughout the training, there may be things that you don't understand. For example, why the trainer is instructing you to do it that way or setting rules that seem insignificant. If you don't understand, the best thing you can do is ask.

I guarantee that they tell you things to set you up for success. Having worked with your specific assistance dog for a while and with their dog training experience, they may tell you things because they know how your dog ticks. For example, when the dog gets too excited, what to do to help this dog regain focus. The things trainers instruct you on are intentional, to help you build up your toolbox.

They also set rules for a reason. The trainer will probably send you home with your dog for the first time with a list of rules on what you can and cannot do initially. This typically includes the instruction to lie low the first few days. You, however, are probably excited, and that's the last thing you want to do.

However, this rule is to help set the dog up for success more so than you. Lying low initially will help the dog get comfortable in your home before being asked to perform skills there.

Additionally, the rules typically have to do with safety for you or the dog or maintaining an appropriate progression of training and bonding. For example, you may feel like these rules are making you move too slowly. Too many times, people who start the process of getting an assistance dog try to do too much too fast. From experience, this will not help you be a successful team in the long run, and by setting these rules, the trainers are trying to guide you into long-term success.

It is completely understandable and okay to not understand why your trainer is instructing you a certain way. You don't have to trust the instructor blindly. Ask why, and the instructor should be able to tell you.

Additionally, there will be times during training when you don't understand what your trainer is telling you or asking of you. Expect this. After all, you are learning to work and communicate with an animal and build a toolbox of resources at the same time. If you don't understand what your instructor is saying, ask for an explanation in a different way. All handlers learn differently, and trainers should be able to explain things in different words and techniques to help you understand.

Please don't feel shy about asking questions. If you are uncertain about something, anything, just ask. There is no such thing as a stupid question when learning something new. Write your questions down if you need to so you don't forget before the next training session. Make sure you have a relationship with your trainer where you feel comfortable asking what may seem like silly questions.

Asking questions even after the initial training period is over is incredibly valuable because the trainer's eyes won't be on the dog nearly as frequently; therefore, the trainer can't intervene if they see something that needs correcting. However, at this point, you should feel relatively comfortable with what is okay and normal for your dog. If you have a question about your dog's behavior or training, no matter how mundane, ask.

It is important that you don't wait too long to ask a question or let an undesirable behavior continue, as you don't want your dog to practice bad behaviors over time. By communicating your concerns or questions earlier, you will have a better chance of stopping the undesirable behavior before your dog has thoroughly learned it and created a routine out of it. It is more difficult to disrupt a routine the more times it has been practiced. For example, a dog that is jumping on people who come to the door. This behavior is much easier to correct when it has only been practiced once, compared to when it has been practiced every time someone has come to the door for a week, a month, etc. Therefore, even after training ends, make sure to stay in communication with your trainer. However, remember that you are most likely not your trainer or organization's only client; therefore, when asking a question, be patient, and don't expect an immediate response.

If you are not willing to be open and honest in your communication with the organization or trainer, then an assistance dog as a tool to mitigate your disability won't be successful.

Your best interests in mind

The last thing to consider is whether the organization or trainer has your best interests in mind. If you have done your research on their quality, cost, and training style, location, and strategy and feel comfortable with their communication, you should have a good idea whether they have your best interests at heart. Or is it all about their financial wallet or moving dogs out of training?

Having your best interests in mind should mean they are willing to work with you, your abilities, and your disabilities as one—adapting their methods or styles to you (to a point) so you can have the best possible outcome for success with an assistance dog. This does not mean that they fundamentally change their program for you. If this is necessary, you will want to consider an organization or trainer whose specialty or methods cater to your specific needs.

At all times your trainer should also have the dog's welfare as a priority. The trainer should be looking out for the dog, confirming that you can properly care for and provide for the dog, creating a mutually beneficial relationship. This is typically seen in the thoroughness of the interview and the matching process.

Although their goals should be to have your best interests in mind and your dog's best interests, unfortunately, these do not always align. This can be very challenging for the organization or trainer, and I ask that you have grace with them, as they are trying to do right by two living beings when making decisions.

The best way to make sure that you will be successful with an assistance dog is to set yourself up for success by choosing the organization or trainer that is best for you.

Takeaways

Getting and working with an assistance dog is a big decision. *How* you get an assistance dog is also a big decision. This section has hopefully provided you with further understanding of the importance of determining whether you want to train your own assistance dog or train with a fully trained assistance dog. When making this decision, it is important to consider your abilities and disabilities, tolerance for puppies and untrained dogs, the time, effort, patience, resiliency, and consistency needed.

It is also important to understand the reasons why dogs may not be suitable for assistance dog work. Not all dogs want to be assistance dogs or have the physical health to work, and that's okay.

Finally, you should have a better understanding of how to vet an organization or trainer to ensure that they can help you be as successful as possible when working with an assistance dog. To set yourself and your future dog up for success, do your research and ask questions.

🐾 Do you believe you will be more successful with a pretrained assistance dog or by training one yourself? Why?

🐾 Can you add any more pros and cons to your list?

Part 3 learning objectives

After reading this section you should be able to…

- determine which avenue of training is most likely to lead to success for you.
- recognize why not all dogs want to be assistance dogs.
- identify the pros and cons for each training avenue.
- determine how to choose the right assistance dog organization or trainer for your needs.

CHAPTER 14

Closing remarks

Assistance dogs are incredible pieces of medical equipment. They are exceptionally versatile and can assist with many disabilities. However, they are not the right tool for everyone. Before you commit to this journey, it is imperative that you know whether an assistance dog can be trained to assist you to mitigate the effects of your disability and whether you can form a mutually beneficial partnership with the dog.

I hope this book helped you complete step one—deciding whether this journey is right for you.

If you have determined that an assistance dog cannot assist your disability or you cannot form a mutually beneficial relationship with them, unfortunately, they are not the right tool for you. *Determining this is also a big step!* If this journey is not right for you, it is important to know this before you have invested significant time, energy, and money into this process.

Additionally, an assistance dog is just one of many types of assistance that could mitigate the effect of your disability. If it happens that you have realized that an assistance dog isn't the feasible path for you *at this moment*, you can explore other options or prepare your life so an assistance dog could be feasible in the future.

If you decide to get an assistance dog regardless, you will spend your partnership fraught with challenges, fighting an uphill battle. I do not recommend this for anyone.

But what if the opposite is true? What if you now believe an assistance dog can assist to mitigate the effects of your disability and that you can form a mutually beneficial relationship with them? Congratulations! Take a moment to pat yourself on the back and maybe scratch your belly or behind your ear. This is a big step. Remember, though, that this is a journey, and you are only at the beginning. It can lead to benefits that will change your life. They include providing physical benefits through trained skills that mitigate the effects of your disability, as well as various psychological and social benefits.

These benefits can be your reality. I have seen handlers *blossom* time and time again when working with an assistance dog. The ones that blossom the brightest have taken the time to prepare and set realistic expectations for themselves physically, mentally, and emotionally for both the possible benefits and the demanding challenges they may experience when working with an assistance dog. Again, I will remind you that it won't be an easy journey.

Even if an assistance dog is the right tool for you, if your expectations are not appropriate or realistic, then you will hinder your ability to successfully work with your dog. This proved true in the research conducted for my doctoral dissertation, as well as in extensive experience working with people who have various disabilities. Based on this experience, I determined that the more prepared handlers are and the more realistic their expectations, the more successful the handlers will be in working with their assistance dog as a team.

After reading this book, working through the questions presented throughout, and discussing with your support system, I hope you have a better understanding of whether an assistance dog is the right tool for you. *It is incredibly important that you think through this journey carefully.* After all, assistance dogs are neither robots nor magical unicorns. They are first and foremost dogs.

ABOUT THE AUTHOR

Jennifer Gravrok has been studying and working with assistance dog organizations, clients, and assistance dogs since 2016. She completed her PhD in December 2019 at La Trobe University, where she studied the benefits and challenges that first-time assistance dog handlers experience. She worked with people who received a variety of types of assistance dogs from different organizations around Australia and the world. Her doctoral thesis was awarded the Nancy Millis Award for exceptional merit, rated in the top 5 percent of theses examined.

During this time, she also did volunteer work, assisting in raising and training numerous dogs at different stages, from puppies to fully trained assistance dogs.

Since then, she has also worked for two assistance dog organizations in the United States, where she predominantly worked with handlers. In this, she has involved herself in all aspects of the journey: interviewing prospective clients, assisting in the matching process between client and dog, preparing and teaching clients how to work with their matched assistance dog, and problem-solving ongoing challenges they experienced years after placement.

Throughout, she has collected scientific research and anecdotal notes about the challenges handlers experience and information that clients have stated they wished they knew before partnering with an assistance dog. In *Understanding Assistance Dogs*, she has compiled these benefits, challenges, and experiences for your benefit, aiming to share the true journey of getting an assistance dog with the world.

What's next?

To set yourself up for success in the next stages of your journey, make yourself aware of the challenges involved in working with an assistance dog so you can set realistic expectations for yourself and your dog. To learn more about this, go to www.understandingassistancedogs.com, where you will find additional helpful resources.

Stay tuned for future books to assist you on this journey!

Can you help?

If you found benefit from this book, please pay it forward for other prospective assistance dog handlers and leave an honest review wherever you purchased the book.

Join me on social media

Instagram: @UnderstandingAssistanceDogs
Facebook: Understanding Assistance Dogs

www.ingramcontent.com/pod-product-compliance
Lightning Source LLC
Chambersburg PA
CBHW070702130626
46553CB00005B/1800